ARE WE LOSING
AMERICA

The Erosion of Our Freedom and How It Can Be Stopped

ARE WE LOSING AMERICA

The Erosion of Our Freedom and How It Can Be Stopped

PATRICK G. SMITH

ACW Press
Ozark, AL 36360

Are We Losing America?
Copyright ©2005 Patrick G. Smith
All rights reserved

Cover Design by Alpha Advertising
Interior Design by Pine Hill Graphics

Packaged by ACW Press
1200 HWY 231 South #273
Ozark, AL 36360
www.acwpress.com
The views expressed or implied in this work do not necessarily reflect those of ACW Press. Ultimate design, content, and editorial accuracy of this work is the responsibility of the author(s).

CREDIT LINE
Excerpts from pages 381-387 from STANDING FIRM by DAN QUAYLE
Copyright © 1994 by J. Danforth Quayle
Reprinted by permission of HarperCollins Publishers

Library of Congress Cataloging-in-Publication Data
(Provided by Cassidy Cataloguing Services, Inc.)

Smith, Patrick G.

   Are we losing America? / Patrick G. Smith. -- 1st ed. -- Ozark, AL :
   ACW Press, 2005.

     p. ; cm.

     ISBN-13: 978-932124-69-9
     ISBN-10: 1-932124-69-1
     Includes bibliographical references.

     1. National characteristics, American. 2. Nationalism--United
   States. 3. Patriotism--United States. 4. Mass media--Influence.
   5. Mass media and culture--United States. I. Title.

JC311 .S56 2005
320.54/0973--dc22   0512

Printed in the United States of America.

Table of Contents

Introduction

Americans today are worried about terrorists destroying America. Some may even worry about invading armies from nations or groups of nations that have far greater populations than we do. Personally I do not believe that terrorists, or invading armies, or even weapons of mass destruction would be able to conquer the United States.

But there is a far more insidious enemy that has done more to weaken us than any foreign power ever has. If this force is allowed to continue, for the most part unopposed by the majority of Americans, then the America that we have all grown up knowing and loving will be eradicated from the face of the Earth. This is the enemy within.

Cancer cells are not viruses or bacteria from outside the body. Cancer cells are a person's own individual cells that "selfishly" reproduce without regard to the well-being of the body as a whole. Eventually they take away all the nutrients the body needs for sustenance, sacrificing the healthy cells for their own wants until the body dies, inadvertently killing the cancer cells themselves as well. Ironically, just like the cancer cells, these people probably don't even realize the totality of the destruction they will cause and they certainly don't realize that they will fall with the rest of us.

If I wanted to make sure that the USA was history before 2025, I would do four main things: (1) destroy the traditional American culture, (2) erode capitalism away in favor of socialism, (3) eliminate the Christian foundation that this country was built on and (4) implement the homosexual agenda, principally as outlined in the Gay Rights Platform of 1972.

Fifty years ago, if someone had stated that this four-pronged attack on America would even be attempted, people would have said he was crazy. As of the year 2005, all four of these things are over halfway completed. If this trend is not reversed, if it continues unabated, our children could be raising their children in a third world country occupying the space that used to be called The United States of America.

This book will go into these four main areas as well as tangent areas that have contributed to the rise of these destructive trends and the programmed indifference of the majority of the population.

The reason I, just an average American, got fired up enough to write this book was that I read Bernard Goldberg's book, *Bias*, and then read the reviews in several of the conservative publications I receive. They all said the same thing: Good book, but why is it selling so well when everybody already knows all this? I was shocked. They don't know! They believe that this is all common knowledge. But I am a blue collar worker, although I am admittedly a blue collar worker with a four-year degree in history from a major university, and the people I work with every day were either surprised by what Goldberg had to say, or were so programmed by the liberal establishment that they just did not believe him.

I decided to write a book that would try to wake up the vast majority of Americans to the surging struggle going on between those that would destroy us and those trying to preserve America. Ironically, those who consider themselves moderates are an essential key to whether America survives or not. If they can be convinced that although they can stay in middle on most issues, they must choose sides on a few that are either life-giving or lethal, then they will determine the outcome of this new kind of civil war. Hopefully, many conservatives will glean some new light herein and some liberals who simply follow their leaders will learn enough to know to quit the left and join the right in this unbelievably important war of values, the results of which are more far reaching than most people could possibly imagine.

Most importantly, this book will tell you how to go about saving America. No single soldier saved the world in World War II, but every soldier was important. It will be the same now.

Every little action you take will add to the actions of millions of other patriots and the cumulative effect will insure that your children's children will also live in the land of the free.

This book could be a turning point when Americans take back America. If you agree that most of the principles (you don't have to agree with every detail) in this book could start to bring back lost freedoms and rights to average Americans and prevent the further erosion of them, and that the simple actions individuals can take to get that liberty back for themselves should be promoted, then I ask you to help in this peaceful revolution.

After reading part, or all, of this book, please order five copies to give or sell to friends, relatives, coworkers, acquaintances or strangers. (As a matter of fact, for every four you buy at $17.95 apiece, I'll throw in the fifth one free if you use the address below to order.) Hopefully, the recipients will do the same. Assuming that the majority of people who read this will do only the minimum (a commitment of about 15 minutes four times a year), then we need millions of people to read it for it to do the maximum good. Thank you. Send check or money order to:

Patrick G. Smith
Are We Losing America? Order
P.O. Box 8155
Scottsdale, Arizona 85252-8155

For credit card orders or bookstore orders, please use the 800 or 877 number on the order form at the back of the book. For single copy orders, follow additional shipping instructions on the order form.

Chapter 1

Traditional
American Culture

The traditional American culture is rapidly ceasing to exist. Formerly, when immigrants came to this country, they were required to learn the language, history and culture of our country to become citizens. Most people coming here were eager to do so, for they intuitively realized that America was the unique land of opportunity and freedom, and that those precious treasures sprang from our traditions.

They were welcome to keep their own culture (think of Chinatown, Little Tokyo, the Saint Patrick's Day Parade, Cinco de Mayo, etc.) as long as they learned ours as well.

Today, they don't have to bother. We've hired teachers to teach their children in the parents' native tongues and we'll even print up voting ballots in their languages. Plus, we've removed most of our history, traditions and culture from the curriculum of our schools so that our own children don't learn it, let alone theirs. Most of it has been replaced by feminism, political correctness and multiculturalism. Before some people jump to erroneous conclusions, let me emphasize that America has room to honor and practice all cultural traditions (as long as they are not illegal or immoral by our laws) but we must be careful to preserve our culture *instead of replacing it* with other cultures if we are to retain the benefits of that culture: human rights, freedom, wealth and power. If we do not teach new citizens our culture, they will have no choice but to keep the cultural traits that led to the social structure (dictatorship, poverty, lack of individual rights, lack of rule of just laws, etc.) that made their former country unfit to live in. (An example of other countries' cultural traits was revealed by Major Jim Murphy during the rebuilding of Baghdad after the second Iraq war. "It is pretty much expected in this culture that you will make kickbacks and practice cronyism and nepotism. Practices in public life that would get you prosecuted in the U.S. are almost a norm here."[1]) And then, with more and more such people with those traits, our country will become more and more like their former countries. When multiculturalism *replaces* American culture, we all lose. Without traditional American culture and the English language unifying the USA, we will become a bunch of warring little cultures, which will eventually weaken us, and could even destroy us. ("Every kingdom divided against itself will be ruined, and every city or household divided against itself will not stand.")

In late August of 2005, there was a news story on a school that had a number of children whose families had fled from Somalia because of the endemic violence there. In one incident, one of the grade school girls they spoke to had been shot in the stomach by a man in her old country. During an interview with her teacher the instructor said that is was not her job to Americanize these children. This is a very politically correct statement; after all, our culture is no better than theirs, right? However, the practical effect of not Americanizing these kids is they will have no alternative but to retain many traits of a culture in which it is considered normal to shoot an elementary school girl in the stomach, if her family is viewed as on the enemy's side.

---

1 Zinsmeister, Karl. "The Search for Citizens" *Focus on the Family Citizen* June 2004: 26-27.

I read an article that quoted many statistics about how little our young people are taught about American history, but I think the last statistic says it all: Zero percent of America's top 55 colleges have an American history requirement.[2]

Have you ever wondered why it seems like over half the people in the world, if given a choice, would rather live here than where they were raised? It is because the USA is the freest, richest, and best country in the world. I didn't mention the most powerful country in the world, because that is not why most people want to come here. (Think of Nazi Germany winning WWII and being the most powerful nation in the world. Do you think that people would be breaking down the borders to get in?)

Many aliens go through hoops and wait for years to get legal status in this country. They are very welcome within the quotas we set. Then there are those who don't pay any attention to our laws and come in illegally. Around twenty years ago we put the lawbreakers ahead of all those who did everything required of them and gave those that were here illegally amnesty! This has exacerbated the illegal alien problem exponentially. There were around eight million illegal aliens then; there are around twenty million now. Many of those illegal aliens have since become citizens, learning that breaking the law has great rewards, more so than going through the proper procedure. I cannot help but wonder how those who did everything the way we told them to and waited years must feel, when we passed over them to make lawbreakers take their place. Furthermore, I can hardly believe that as of this writing, we are talking about doing this all over again! We must learn that as long as you reward criminal behavior, crime will increase.

PROPAGANDA

It is absolutely amazing how effective the propaganda ministry, I mean the major media, is in completely brainwashing a huge portion of the American population. When I was young, in the 1950s and 1960s, we knew that disarming our honest citizens would turn us into a nation of victims unnecessarily; borrowing

---

2 Veith, Gene Edward. "The conservationist" *World Magazine* 29 Jan. 2005: 22.

the funds out of Social Security to spend on political pork was foolish, killing babies who were inconvenient through abortion was immoral (and since those citizens we aborted would not be able to pay into Social Security and other retirement funds, there would not be enough money coming in to allow our generation to retire), and homosexuality was a sexual deviancy. Yet, through brainwashing by the liberal establishment, all of these things are now considered controversial at best and downright wrong at worst. Some of the subtleties of this are explained by Gene Edward Veith:

"Radicals used to put their hope in revolution, but in the post-Soviet era, the radical left has shifted to the advice of Marxist theorist Antonio Gramsci: Take over the culture. This can be done by shaping the way people think, their values and worldview.

"...the usual group of radicals are adopting a tone of high moral indignation in scolding America for its ethical shortcomings. ...They reject personal morality but believe in social morality. Holding the right political beliefs enables them to feel self-righteousness, without the trouble of actually being righteous. ...Genuine morality, of course, has *both* a personal and social dimension."[3]

We all have to quit letting the constant drone of political correctness we are immersed in every day push our brains into neutral and stop our critical thinking processes. There are reasons why traditional American culture held certain beliefs before the post-modern, politically correct era took over. We forget those reasons and abandon that culture at the risk of losing all its accomplishments: freedom, liberty, wealth, etc.

HONESTY REALLY IS THE BEST POLICY

"When there is a lack of honor in government, the morals of the whole people are poisoned. There is no such thing as a no-man's land between honesty and dishonesty. Our strength lies in spiritual concepts. It lies in public sensitiveness to evil. Our greatest danger is not from invasion by foreign armies. Our dangers are

---

3 Veith, Gene Edward "Saddam chic" *World Magazine*. 15 Mar 2003: 13.

that we may commit suicide from within by complaisance with evil, or by public tolerance of scandalous behavior."[4]

Our society was built on honesty and integrity. Yes, the power of political position has corrupted some of our politicians; but compared to many other cultures, our officials are almost squeaky clean. Elsewhere, tens of thousands of citizens die each year directly because of the corruption of their leaders. However, a few more years of our society drifting to the political left and we may no longer be any better than those societies.

When I was in high school, we had a foreign exchange student from a certain South American country. He was amazed and bewildered by the wealth, the freedom and the honesty we enjoy here. When I did not understand, he said something like this:

"You have entire industries that could not exist in my country. You have, for instance, those coin-operated newspaper stands where people put in a coin, lift the cover, take out one paper, and replace the cover. In my country, the first person would put in the coin, lift the cover, take all the papers out, go about a block away, and sell the papers for half price."

The above scenario would have been anathema to most Americans in the 1960s. We've come a long way in that direction in the ensuing years though. Someone at work was mentioning how he wanted a certain new computer program that had recently come out. Then his wife looked for it, but instead of buying it, came back with the news that it cost fifty dollars! He said to us: "So I was smart. I just went down to (a certain store), rented the program, took it home, burned a copy and all it cost was almost nothin' for the blank CD." When I mentioned something about piracy, he just said something vague about "everybody does it." (Didn't certain types of disreputable guys use that line to get naive girls into bed with them?) He quickly added: "And besides, Bill Gates can afford it!" I said, "Oh, really? Then since you and your wife earn over $100,000 a year, you wouldn't mind if someone poorer than you stole your TV, DVD or computer, since you have so much more than they do?" Yes, it really is similar.

---

4 Herbert Hoover, as reported in the Presidential Prayer Team newsletter: 29 Jan. 2004.

Later on I realized that his "Gates can afford it!" argument is further destroyed by the fact that Gates is not the one pirates are stealing from. Bill will pass the cost of piracy onto those who buy the programs. My friend is actually stealing from me! What you and I pay for the software that comes with the computers we buy and the additional programs we buy is much higher than it would be without piracy.

When he pirated some other registered material off the Internet and I mentioned it, he switched tactics. "But I didn't pirate it; someone else did, and posted it on the Internet." So I guessed that if a poor person stole his computer, with his name and address on it, and just left it on the sidewalk and someone else picked it up and didn't return it, that would be OK?

Joel Belz wrote an editorial about the conversation of two families at the table behind him at a motel restaurant. The parents, in front of their children, discussed how they had been undercharged at a Target store by a factor of ten and did not let the clerk know; they snuck an overage boy who was a ringer onto a Little League team to get a winning season; one man seemingly stretched the truth to get out of paying more child support for the kids he deserted; and a mother at the table was proud of her daughter for getting around college dorm rules by moving in with her boyfriend in the dorm she wanted to move into. About this Mr. Belz wrote:

"We're not talking here about graduate-level morality. We're not asking whether this society has what it takes to discuss sophisticated ethical issues. We're not even suggesting that our culture in this case swear an allegiance to our version of biblical morality; we're looking for little more here than an elementary understanding of the Golden Rule. These are kindergarten issues—and if we can't master them, who on earth do we think we are talking about the ethics of stem-cell research, just-war theory, end-of-life issues, and abortion?"[5]

My greatest fear is not that we no longer have the strength of our convictions, but that we no longer have convictions.

---

5 Joel Belz, "Flunking Kindergarten" *World Magazine*, 13 Nov 2004: 6.

"Honesty" and "integrity" have been replaced by "everything is relative" and "it's OK as long as I get mine." We must understand that such things, over time, and gaining acceptance with more and more people, will have a cumulative and devastating effect on our society.

It is not one giant termite that causes a building to collapse. It is thousands of tiny termites that destroy what many worked so hard to build, and someone has to work a lifetime to pay for. America is that building. When we pirate, steal, lie and cheat or stand by and do nothing when others try to remove our Christian foundation; or judges usurp power and destroy our freedoms and we do not call our Congressmen and demand those judges be impeached, we are one of those termites.

WHICH WAY ARE WE HEADED?

During WWII many of the movie stars like Jimmy Stewart, Clark Gable and Audie Murphy gave up their glamorous careers to risk their lives to fight for what America stood for. Abbott and Costello, as well as Carol Lombard and others, did war bond drives to raise money for the war effort. People like these are rarely even allowed to start careers in Hollywood today. These people had their own problems and weaknesses, but they did what they thought was right at great risk to themselves.

We are in the tremendous process of lowering our standards and calling it freedom.

I am reminded of a study that I became aware of that compared both Christian and public colleges' students and their moral standards in the 1950s compared to the 1980s. This was in regard to traditional moral standards: No sex before marriage, being honest is always right, etc. It was found that the religious schools of the 1950s had higher morals than the secular colleges of the 1950s and the religious schools of the 1980s had higher morals than the secular schools of the 1980s. This finding didn't shock anybody. But what was interesting was that the secular schools of the 1950s had higher morals than the religious schools of the 1980s. Since the biblical standards on which religious schools are based hadn't changed, researchers were at a loss as to why this should be so.

When he was interviewed, a young student came up with a very plausible answer. He reasoned that as long as the Christian students felt that their morals were slightly higher than the morals of the kids in secular schools, they were OK. Therefore, as the morals in the public schools went down, the morals in the religious schools followed in the same direction, resulting in the surprising finding mentioned above.

When we Americans assume that no matter how low our standards go (whether moral, quality of life, work ethic, self-discipline, education, etc.), America will always remain strong, we are like the immature, but legally adult-age person who inherits a large sum of money and lives off the principal of the inheritance without bringing in any of his own income. Eventually the inheritance gets used up and he is wiped out, in poverty. When we lower our standards, we spend our American inheritance.

Traditional American culture is rich in honesty, integrity, morality, a sense of fair play.

Sex has always been held in great esteem, but tended to be reserved for marriage. For instance, in a Barna Poll taken in 2002 and compared with previous years, it was discovered that the percentage of people in the US who believe that premarital sex is morally wrong was: 1969, 68 percent; 1987, 46 percent; 1992, 33 percent; 2002, 42 percent. I hypothesize that the reason that the percentage is on the rise again, after such a great decline, is that people are finally starting to realize the consequences of the sexual revolution of the 1960s.

INDIVIDUALISM

Another trait of our culture is individualism, both in expression and in self-reliance. From beatniks and hippies of the 1950s and 1960s to businessmen and housewives, we were all our own individual persons. Since the liberal establishment took over, though, now we are all to be politically correct or we are troublemakers. They tell us we must conform! I just don't believe that most Americans want to be told how to think, act and speak.

The other half of individualism is self-reliance. We are told that government must be ever-expanding so that it can take care of all of us. No mention of the fact that the more government programs there are, the more power the individual must give up so the power of our "representatives" can grow as the government grows. There has to be a point at which the municipalities become so bloated that they suck the life out of the private sector by taxing it out of existence. Then the source of all these goodies is gone. The Feds, states, etc. can no longer take care of us and we will have forgotten how to take care of ourselves.

DUTY

For reasons far divergent from the purpose of this book, inner-city black neighborhoods have preceded white suburbs in veering away from the traditional American family. In 1965 Daniel Patrick Moynihan was soundly criticized for his conclusions in his paper "The Negro Family: the Case for National Action." He said: "A community that allows a large number of young men to grow up in broken families, dominated by women, never acquiring any stable relationships to male authority, never acquiring any set of rational expectations about the future—that community asks for and gets chaos." With the breakdown of suburban families, what he said in 1965 about the inner city is totally applicable to suburbia today. The disregard for duty to the spouses we sleep with and the children we create has led to a societal mess that we will not even realize the severity of until this next generation is in charge.

There is also duty that we owe to the American culture that many ungrateful people disregard. A case in point is Columbia University Anthropology Professor Nicholas De Genova, who said, "The only true heroes are those who find ways that help defeat the US military. I personally would like to see a million Mogadishus."[6] In Mogadishu, Somalia, eighteen US soldiers were killed and dragged through the streets, at least one naked. Old Nick hopes for "a very different world than the one in which we live—a world where the US would have no place."[7] He doesn't seem very grateful for the opportunities that America has provided for him to reach a place of prominence.

---

6 Olasky, Marvin. "Worse Than War" *World Magazine* 12 April 2003: 7.
7 Ibid

Now, I believe totally in De Genova's freedom to believe what he wants and his right to say what he thinks. But why would any American college student ever sign up for his classes again? Even if it is a required course, there are usually other teachers teaching it as well, or you can get your counselor to authorize a suitable substitute class. Only liberals believe that their right to free speech comes with an iron-clad guarantee that no one else will exercise their rights and not patronize that person anymore. Oddly, liberals do not believe that conservatives have the same guarantee. For instance, when the Florida Orange Juice industry advertised on the Rush Limbaugh show, liberals thought nothing of calling for a nationwide boycott of Florida Orange products; but watch their reaction anytime a conservative suggests similar remedies.

"Western intellectuals demand freedom in their own lifestyles, but they undermine the ideologies that have given them that freedom.

"...most Christians and social conservatives are more willing than pro-tolerance liberals to fight against those who execute gays, enslave women, censor entertainment, and stamp out every freedom....

"...Soviet communism collapsed not only for military reasons but because by the end of the century, its ideology was refuted not by arguments but by facts. ...morality and freedom not only can coexist but support each other."[8]

INTEGRITY

Traditionally, an American will do what he knows to be right, even when he does not like doing it. But one of the main signs that our culture is disappearing is that our integrity is weakening. To show this decline, I'll take an example from work. A fellow worker called over the radio for someone to come assist him. The guy I was working with insisted that neither of us should leave our assigned work area to help him.

---

8 Veith, Gene Edward. "Praise the Lord, pass the ammo" *World Magazine* 25 Oct. 2003: 10.

When I said I was going to help the guy anyway, he actually went to the supervisor and had me ordered not to go help. I later learned that he really believed that it was his and my duty to help our fellow worker in such circumstances, but he personally did not like this one guy. He was willing to refrain from doing what he believed to be the right thing to do and prevent someone else from doing the right thing, just because of his personal feelings about an individual. We have to get back to our true American culture, part of which is doing what we know is right, even when we don't want to. Lowering such standards helps to destroy America.

THE LAND OF OPPORTUNITY

The traditional American culture has led to the USA being a land of continuous opportunity. Being born here is a blessing that most people in the world do not understand. They would not believe how good we have it here, even if you told them. A common quote might be, "Yeah, SURE, you Americans don't have to worry about some official from the government showing up and taking you to prison for saying something politically incorrect, like I'm going to believe that." "Yeah, SURE, you can be born crippled in America and still become successful without begging for a living."

For instance: If you were born in India with a severe disability, you would probably spend your life as a beggar on the streets, living in squalor. An acquaintance that went to my church was born with a radical form of premature arthritis. By the time he was a young adult he was very limited in physical capability. As an adult he had to walk on crutches. But in the USA he got therapy, got an accounting degree, worked hard, had a good job as an accountant, wore nice suits and lived quite well. Such stories are relatively common in the United States, but almost unheard of in the majority of countries in the world.

MORALITY

To understand what traditional American culture is, it is good to look at what the founding fathers said. Separation of church and state is a modern concept, the way it is misused today. John Adams said: "We have no government armed with power capable of contending with human passions unbridled by morality and religion...Our Constitution was made only for a moral and religious people. It is wholly inadequate to the government of any other."

We must regain our understanding of the importance of morals. For instance, part of our march toward becoming a lower form of life has included a growing acceptance of profanity, obscenity and sacrilege. At one time this sort of language was locker room, or shop talk. Women were shown respect and children's innocence was protected by men ceasing to talk that way in the presence of either. Now, we have let the media deluge us with such language, teachers are told not to notice when students use it, and women have denigrated themselves by adopting it as well.

Actress Patricia Heaton of *Everybody Loves Raymond* fame walked out on her role to introduce a segment of the American Music Awards because of the vile language being used in the show. "I'm no prude, but this was such a vulgar and disgusting show....What was passing for humor basically ranged from stupid to vulgar—and I just thought, 'I'm not going to be part of this.' So I walked out and said, 'Get my car—I'm leaving.'"[9] I applaud her courage. I wish more of us had her guts.

Even Eminem, so famous for being obscene in his singing, who was the biggest winner at this awards ceremony, "has made special, profanity-free versions of his recordings for his 7-year-old daughter Hailie. One wants to ask him, 'If you want to shelter your own daughter from this kind of language, why are you putting it out for other people's kids?'"[10]

We have to learn to say, "Enough." If you are fed up with the media's part in this, I suggest you contact Parents Television Council listed in Appendix 1. They put pressure on the FCC to enforce standards in the media. To those who say that this is an infringement on freedom of speech, please remember that

9 Veith, Gene Edward "Clearing the Air" *World Magazine* 8 Feb 2003: 11.
10 Ibid.

freedoms are a balance of your freedom versus your freedom infringing on other people's freedoms. Freedom is not license and we owe it to those who came before us to show our fellow Americans the dignity and respect that is due the citizens of the greatest country in the world. We should respect ourselves enough to discipline our tongues and learn how to speak properly. In normal daily situations vulgar language has no positive influence, no benefit; it just denigrates the user and belittles the listener.

FAMILIES

Traditionally our family structure tended to be a man working for the money needed and a woman raising the children and tending the home, running the errands. This is harder to do than it was in yesteryear. Audrey Meadows, in her book, *Love, Alice,* said, "Why was one salary enough in the fifties and two don't quite make it in the nineties? Who changed the rules and why? Did we ever have a vote to make life harder?"[11] She doesn't seem to be able to come up with an answer. Even with the Reagan and George W. Bush tax cuts, taxes are still a far larger percentage of income than they were in the 1950s. I have a hypothesis: As government programs are increased, government grows. Then taxes go up. Therefore, the number of hours of work per week, per family, needed to pay those taxes (and pay living expenses) has gone from 40 to 50 hours of work per week in the 1950s to 80 to 100 hours per week today.[12] Therefore, increased taxes could explain it.

Unless we start a *serious* program of reducing the size of government, we are stuck with this situation. If we choose not to do this, then to reinstate the old division of family labor back into our society (if that is our personal preference) will take more discipline than in prior generations. A battle plan might be for young people to postpone sex and marriage, get a good education, training, or start in a business, get established in your career, and get married after you have a firm grip on a good start in life. Then when the babies come along, the wife can quit work and stay home if she chooses to do so.

---

11 Meadows, Audrey *Love, Alice.* NY, NY: Crown Publishers, Inc., 1994: 182.
12 My own cynical analysis, I am quoting no authority.

Many will say, "Why can't the man stay home?" Perhaps some can. But in my experience, women are more multi-tasked, nurturing, and patient than men and those are traits you need in spades to be the main person raising a child.

BELIEF IN GOD MAKES US GOOD

Traditional American culture has always included the belief in God and the moral conviction that we will eventually answer for our actions to a higher authority. Without this conviction people tend to gravitate toward becoming a lower form of life. Lower forms of life are never able to continue a great civilization. Alexis de Tocqueville said:

"Not until I went into the churches of America and heard her pulpits, aflame with righteousness, did I understand the secret of her genius and power. America is great because she is good, and if America ever ceases to be good, America will cease to be great." (This quote is often attributed to De Tocqueville, but some students of history say he did not originate it. In my opinion, the statement is nevertheless, true, no matter who said it.)

CONCLUSION

We are no longer good in as many areas as we once were. Modern piracy is way up; executives become parasites, draining off the shareholders profits for themselves; a much larger segment of the male population has gotten into becoming sexual predators; women bear children out of wedlock at an alarming rate, and the men who fathered the kids often skip out on their responsibilities. Some are still honest, some have integrity, some practice abstinence and fidelity; we still try to defend the helpless, most still love the America that was defined by the traditional American culture. But if we continue to decline and allow the traditional American culture to disappear, then, at some point, we will lose our goodness and then we will cease to be great. We must put out the effort to regain what we have lost or we will most certainly lose what we have left.

Chapter 2

Capitalism

The allure of socialism/communism is that it appeals to our sense of getting something for nothing. The government provides health care; we get it free. The government gives pensions; we feel as if we get it for nothing. If we are unemployed, we are given unemployment benefits and it's nice to have that safety net. Many people don't look past that aspect of it.

The government doesn't create wealth. It gets the money from its citizens. The average citizen in the US pays 26 percent of his income is Social Security and income taxes, we being mostly capitalists. Denmark and Germany are examples of socialist economies and their rates for these taxes are 43 percent and 42 percent respectively,[13] even though they earn less and have a lower standard of living than we do. Those who work have to pay for all the extra goodies.

This brings us to a major downside of socialism. If you are "A" and the person next to you is "B," "A" might produce twice as

---

13 "Taxes" The World Almanac and Book of Facts 2002 Ed.: 154.

much as "B" and instead of profiting, your excess will be split with "B" under pure socialism. After awhile "A" will quit putting out the extra effort until he produces no more than "B." Multiply this effect by millions of people and eventually everyone's standard of living will go down as the more efficient and hard working people lower their standards.

Capitalism has made us the richest country the world ever dreamed of. For instance, Germany, France and Japan all have per capita GDP of about $23,000.[14] In the USA it is over $33,900. Television sets per 1,000 people in each country are: Germany 571; France 606; Japan 708; USA 847. Keep in mind that these other countries are among the richest, next to us, in the world. Taking Argentina as an example of the next tier down the ladder, they have a per capita GDP of $10,000 and have 289 TV sets per 1000 people. Below that are the third world countries, the citizens of which cannot even understand how the average American lives, let alone dream of attaining that standard. The vast majority of countries are in those two lower tiers.

SOCIALISM

Despite all the evidence that our capitalistic system is far superior to any other system, many of our elected officials keep legislating more socialism. For instance, people dream of totally socializing medicine in this country because medical costs are so high. And yet, people come here to get medical attention from countries that have socialized medicine because the line (or queue) for treatment is so long that many would die before they could be treated.

When government becomes too big, with tentacles in too many directions, it becomes socialistic, draining the economy to feed itself.

Maybe an example of how the US government has grown will be edifying: In the mid-1890s J. P. Morgan became the richest man in the world. With his net worth, compared to the US budget of his day, he could have paid to run the government for

---

14 "Nations of the World" *The World Almanac and Book of Facts* 2002 Ed.: 767.

over twenty years. A hundred years later, in the mid-1990s, Bill Gates became the richest man in the world. With his net worth and the US budget what they were then, he could have paid to run the government for about six weeks.

Either today's rich are very poor, or our government has become super-morbidly obese.

AVOIDING SHORTAGES

If there is a correlation coefficient between how much work a man or woman is willing to do and how much they can count on being justly compensated in proportion to that effort, people will become far more efficient and productive than under any system that ensures that all will be equally compensated, no matter how much or how little time, effort and risk they put into their work. If we don't reward productivity, people will cease to be productive. If we reward laziness, people will get lazier.

Honesty is extremely important in capitalism. If companies cannot count on being proportionately compensated for the effort they put out, they tend to go out of business. We all lose access to their product. If enough people shoplift, stores go out of business and that area loses services. If enough people pirate music, software, CDs, DVDs and videos, people will eventually stop producing the wonderful things we all enjoy. If a huge percentage of us excuse away our tendency to take what we have not paid for (and were supposed to), we could someday have plenty of money to buy anything we want, but the products will not be available for purchase, or even theft, anymore. This type of shortage has already happened in other countries.

For example, I was talking to my friend, Joe, who is a naturalized American, originally from the former Soviet Union. I was mentioning how I had won a large prize in a raffle. He said that in the Soviet Union he had won a raffle and got a refrigerator. Yet, he kept on mentioning having to pay full price for it. Finally, he explained that these raffles just give you the right to buy whatever you "win" because you could not buy a great many things at any price because of all the shortages. Another acquaintance of mine from the same country remembered that her parents bought new furniture and had to wait four months for delivery.

In the USSR, communism led to all the shortages. In the USA, dishonesty can ensure that we wind up with shortages as well.

CEOs CAN BE PIRATES TOO

And while we're at it, let's look at the other side of the spectrum on the necessity of honesty—honesty at the top of the commercial food chain. I owned several different companies' stocks in the 1980s and 1990s. I believe that I read through more of the paperwork than the average stock owner does and noticed an alarming trend. I found that most of the boards of directors and CEOs of many of the companies were voting themselves enormous bonuses, totaling hundreds of millions of dollars per company. (I use the term "bonuses" generically; it is meant to include stock options and other means of getting more money to the top executives than just their salaries.)

Later, a financial magazine published an article on this growing problem. When they interviewed the executives they stated that these bonuses were tied to the stock prices, so as long as the stocks went up, they were being justly compensated for their work. Then the recession that started the last six months of the Clinton presidency caused stock prices to tumble for the next two years. But the executives' bonuses were the same as before.

I hypothesized that eventually, if this continued, they would all retire billionaires about the same time that the companies went bankrupt, leaving thousands of people per company unemployed and broke. And I hadn't even thought of the personal disasters caused by the effect on pension plans. A few years after I first made my hypothesis, Montgomery Ward, K-Mart and Enron declared bankruptcy. As I am writing this chapter, this story is suddenly all over the news, so my suggestion that capitalism needs honesty at the top to work has been proven beyond any shadow of a doubt. Company executives, please do not bother giving us the excuse that what you did was completely legal and, therefore, honest. God help us if we have to make a law to cover every person in every situation, every day of our lives. Many things that are not yet technically illegal are still just plain WRONG!

IN A NUTSHELL

"Low taxes spur investment, increase employment, reward productive consumption, boost real wages and expand the tax base. This, plus legal equality, open opportunity and private property rights in capitalist economies most efficiently lifts the working poor into the middle class.

"Quality of life depends on economic productivity, not population density. Dense populations have rising living standards where free market policies foster economic growth. Underproductive socialist systems are 'overpopulated,' with too few workers and too many mouths to feed."[15] (Hong Kong has one of the highest living standards in the world and the population is hundreds of thousands per square mile.)

I know this is an unbelievably short chapter, but that makes it no less important. A fifty-page thesis on capitalism would just bore you. The points are: (A) Communism has never worked. (B) Socialism collapses under ever decreasing productivity; and (C) without everyone's commitment to honesty, everyone eventually loses the vast wealth capitalism has created.

If we want to continue to be the richest country in the world, we have to stop trying to imitate poorer countries by adopting their socialism. Capitalism works!

---

15 Gabler, Mel. Untitled op. ed. *The Mel Gablers' Educational Research Analysts Newsletter*, May 2002: 3.

Chapter 3

Christian Foundation

Though we have been brainwashed to believe otherwise, the United States of America is built on the foundation of Christianity. Most people believe that "Separation of Church and State" is in the Constitution. It is not. This famous phrase is taken out of a letter written by Thomas Jefferson assuring a pastor that there is a "wall of separation between church and state" that would protect the church from being taken over by the federal government. It had nothing to do with protecting Americans or the government from the church.

Despite the constant drum of leftist politicians and left-wing political organizations, there is overwhelming evidence that public demonstrations of our religious heritage are OK. Speaking on this subject and referring to the liberal elite and leftist, activist judges, Dr James Dobson said: "They want to redefine us as a nation and deny the spiritual heritage that brought us to this point. On the United States Supreme Court building are three depictions to the same Ten Commandments and to Moses. The

sergeant of arms has opened every workday since 1777 by shout-
ing, 'God bless the United States and this Court.'"[16]

In "The National Archives building…you have to walk past
the Ten Commandments…." and… "in the chamber of the
House of Representatives…written behind the speaker are the
words 'In God We Trust.'"[17] Also in the chamber is a representa-
tion of Moses. He added that the Liberty Bell has a Scripture
inscribed from the book of Leviticus.

"It is the duty of nations as well as of men to own their
dependence upon the overruling power of God; to confess their
sins and transgressions in humble sorrow, yet with assured hope
that genuine repentance will lead to mercy and pardon; and to
recognize the sublime truth announced in the Holy Scriptures
and proven by all history, that those nations are blessed whose
God is the Lord.

"…But we have forgotten God. We have forgotten the gra-
cious hand which preserved us in peace and multiplied and
enriched and strengthened us, and we have vainly imagined, in
the deceitfulness of our hearts, that all these blessings were produced by some superior wisdom and virtue of our own.
Intoxicated with unbroken success, we have become too self-
sufficient to feel the necessity of redeeming and preserving
grace, too proud to pray to the God that made us.

"It has seemed to me fit and proper that God should be
solemnly, reverently and gratefully acknowledged, as with one
heart and one voice, by the whole American people. I do therefore invite my fellow citizens in every part of the United States,
and also those who are at sea and those who are sojourning in
foreign lands, to set apart and observe the last Thursday of
November as a day of thanksgiving and praise to our beneficent
Father Who dwelleth in the heavens." -Abraham Lincoln,
Thanksgiving Proclamation, 1863.

George Washington wrote to one synagogue: "May the children of the stock of Abraham who dwell in this land continue to

---

16 Dobson, Dr. James. Family News From Dr. James Dobson October 2003: 2.
17 Ibid.

merit and enjoy the good will of the other inhabitants while everyone shall sit in safety under his own vine and fig tree and there shall be none to make him afraid."[18]

This Christian foundation has led us to being the freest nation on Earth. In the United States of America, no Jew, Muslim, Hindu, atheist or New Ager has to worry about the government authorities harassing, fining, arresting, jailing, torturing or killing them because of their beliefs. This is not true in most other countries where foundations are any other religion or even no religion at all. And yet now, after giving so much freedom to others, in the USA, the Christian Church has to continually battle for its rights.

"As long as the country is dominated by Christianity, there will be freedom for everyone to practice whatever religion he or she wants—and freedom to ignore religion altogether. In the absence of a prevailing Christian culture, these precious freedoms are endangered. ...Jews flourish here *because* America is Christian, not in spite of it. ...Freedom of conscience is central to the Christian belief that people are made in God's image.

"The sad history of the 20th century tells us all too clearly that when tyrants stamp out God, or distort religion for their own ends, freedom also dies—with tragic results for people. This is the lesson of Germany under Hitler, the Soviet Union under Stalin, Cambodia under Pol Pot and Iraq under Saddam Hussein. The sad list is written in the blood of the massacred.

"No one suggests that the Christian church, over its long history, is free of its own bloodstains. But these arise largely from the errors of its practitioners, not from the core of its dogma. The two central teachings of the church have been and will always remain: Love God, and love your neighbor as yourself.

"...Christian values are the mainstream in this country. People ought never to be bashful about standing for them, for

---

18 As reported by: Olasky, Marvin in "A Tough Test of Citizenship" *World Magazine* 19 Feb. 2005: 44.

they safeguard freedom for everyone, particularly for those who reject them."[19]

"America needs much prayer, lest it lose its soul." Pope John Paul II.

To give examples of what it is like for Christians in countries with other foundations: (1) In Sudan Christians are massacred, starved, tortured and women and children are sold into slavery. (2) In Indonesia on Christmas Day 2001 a bomb killed nineteen at a church service. (3) A pastor was burned to death with six of his family members in Nigeria for preaching the gospel. (4) In Vietnam the police have burst into Christmas services, torn down decorations and tried to get people to renounce their faith with threats of imprisonment. (5) In Laos seventeen Christians were arrested for attending Christmas services in one incident. Yet, thanks to the liberal bias in our educational institutions, "Only 25% of students believe that the values of the U.S. are superior to the values of other nations. …and 79% of students do not believe the Western Culture is superior to Arab culture."[20]

After a seven-year battle a court decision was decided in 2002 that allowed the Bronx Household of Faith to meet in New York public schools, after school hours, on the same terms as every other group. This, after several prior court cases (some decided by the Supreme Court) had already made this equality of Christian organizations to everybody else patently obvious. Not to mention that all these millions of dollars spent on court cases (both by the legal system and individuals) were already preempted in the 1980s by the equal access law, which in lay-men's terms states simply that if everybody else can use public facilities, then you cannot isolate and exclude a group just because they have a politically incorrect belief system (in most cases traditional Christianity.) To liberals, nothing is settled until it is settled their way.

The obvious point of all this litigation is to financially break the undesirable organization or set new precedents that have the

---

19 Minnery, Tom "A gift for liberals" *Focus on the Family Citizen.* Feb. 2005: 30.
20 Forbes, Steve. Undated fundraising letter for The Heritage Foundation.

effect of reversing the unwanted law or just keep reducing the influence of the perceived evil in our society; perceived evil usually being anyone or anything that is pro-Biblical God, pro-life, pro-Capitalism, pro-morality or pro-traditional American culture.

Since this has already been decided for around twenty years, why do the courts keep accepting these lawsuits that they already know have no merit? Are we getting judges that are totally unfamiliar with the law? Or could it be that they have absolutely no knowledge of past court decisions? This is extremely unlikely. No, what we have here are leftist, activist judges who want to simply reverse precedent, nullify the laws they don't agree with and redesign our society the way they want it to be. It is time for Americans to say that they are fed up with individuals who abuse their power to restructure our society, rejecting the collective wisdom of literally millions of Americans who came before them, and impeach (federal judges) or recall (state judges) these would be mini-dictators. Yes, unlike what you have been told, federal judges can be impeached without them having to break a law first. See the chapter on "The Oligarchy of the Judiciary."

On Sept. 20, 2002 I saw an interview of Christopher Reeve by Barbara Walters. He was a man of great courage, and I would not pretend to be of as strong a will. But strength of will can be used for bad as well as good. At one point, as they were discussing the possibility of harvesting embryos for the purpose of bio-chemically differentiating their stem cells into new nerve cells so people like Reeves could walk again, he said President Bush was too heavily influenced by the religious right and that no religion should be allowed to have any say-so in this matter.

This is rather a terrifying couple of points he is making. He is stating: (1) I'm not going to think about this too deeply, but even if these are human beings, go ahead and destroy them, if they can be used to make me walk again; I just do not care. (2) Religious people should not be allowed to participate in anything important or controversial in our society.

On the one hand, he had the guts to come out and say what most leftists just imply—that Christians should not be allowed any influence in our country—but I cannot admire this bigotry. It was like the time that Phil Donohue said that "we should not allow" people of certain belief systems with which he disagrees or religious beliefs with which he disagrees to get any education past a high school diploma.

Let us compare Christopher Reeves' opinion with that of some of our founding fathers.

"One of the most influential founders of the United States was John Jay, who served in both Continental Congresses and was President Washington's choice to be the first Chief Justice. Jay wrote: "Providence has given to our people the choice of their rulers, and it is the duty, as well as the privilege and interest of our Christian nation to select and prefer Christians for their rulers." Jay was making the case that our nation would best be governed by those who abide by Biblical principles and embrace a Christian worldview, and by those who are committed to a higher standard of personal integrity."[21]

"Daniel Webster said it this way: 'To preserve the government we must also preserve morals. Morality rests on religion; if you destroy the foundation, the superstructure must fall. When the public mind becomes vitiated and corrupt, laws are a nullity and constitutions are waste paper.' What a chilling description of where we are today.

"Patrick Henry articulated a similar caution: 'The great pillars of all government and of social life (are) virtue, morality and religion. This is the armor…and this alone, that renders us invincible.'"[22]

The Chief Justice of the United States from 1811 until 1845 was a man named Joseph Story. He explained the First Amendment like this: "Probably at the time of the adoption of the Constitution and (the First Amendment), the general, if not the universal sentiment in America was, that Christianity ought to receive encouragement from the State so far as was not incompatible with the private rights of conscience and the freedom of

---

21 Munsil, Len. Family Facts-Arizona. Center for Arizona Policy. 9 Sept. 2002: 1.
22 As reported by: Dobson, Shirley in Prayerfully yours, Shirley; *Prayer Lines*, Spring, 2005: 2.

religious worship. Any attempt to level all religions, and to make it a matter of state policy to hold all in utter indifference, would have created universal disapprobation, if not universal indignation. …The real object of the First Amendment was not to countenance, much less to advance Mohammedanism, or Judaism, or infidelity, by prostrating Christianity, but to exclude all rivalry among Christian (denominations) and to prevent any national ecclesiastical patronage of the national government."[23]

We are constantly bombarded by the media and the rest of the liberal establishment with the supposed fact that separation of church and state (a phrase that is contained in no legal document before the twentieth century) means that all public mention of religion must be censored if it is mentioned by anyone on any civil payroll while on duty.

To come to this conclusion, these people have to be totally ignorant of what the founding fathers said about such subjects or they have to believe that our ancestors did not know what they meant by what they said, unless the "separation of church and state" crowd are just plain lying and deceiving the rest of us. (What are the chances?) What the founders said simply meant that there was to be no state religion. The United States of America could not require you to belong to a particular denomination and force you to pay tithes to a state-supported church. That is the only restriction intended by our forefathers. One of the main reasons that universal education was considered desirable was so everyone would be able to read the Bible. The Louisiana Purchase doubled the size of our country and one of the top priorities of our government was to spread Christianity to the new acquisition. Jefferson, the famous deist, was president at the time. He is one of those the anti-Christians always use to show that not all of our founding fathers were Christians; it seems that in spite of this, he did believe that the spread of Christianity was a good thing.

What is one of the main things you hear almost daily about the Republican Party? "They are too much influenced by the

---

23 As reported by Munsil, Len; *Family Facts-Arizona*, Center for Arizona Policy. 9 Sept. 2002: 1.

religious right." (Read Christian citizens here.) But, wait a minute. Around 150,000,000 people in the US belong to various Christian churches. This may come as a shock to people who only get their information from the mainstream media, but all the homosexuals, lesbians, gun controllers, socialists and "throw the borders open" types combined would be less than one-tenth of that, and yet they seem to control the Democratic Party. For this to change, more conservative Democrats need to become Precinct Committeemen and start having an influence on the party, then work their way up from there. The Democratic Party has much good to offer if only the conservative branch would get involved and keep it from being a totally liberal-controlled party.

To give an example of what a precinct committee man can do: In 2003/2004 the Republican establishment in our state was strongly encouraging the reelection of the liberal who was the encumbent national precinct committeeman. He was expected to vote in favor of removing the pro-life plank from the Republican platform. Our district worked hard to recruit conservatives to be PCs and sent over 50 relatively new, conservative PCs to vote in the state convention for the underdog who supported keeping the pro-life plank. Against all odds our guy won by a vote of 289 to 284. As a district, county and state PC myself, it felt wonderful knowing that my vote was one of five that helped strengthen the odds of renewing the pro-life plank.

Censoring free speech and keeping freedom of religion from being practiced in the public arena are favorite ploys of those who would erase our Christian foundation. The paranoia with which the left does this is almost beyond belief.

The Eleventh Circuit Court of Appeals tried the case of *Adler v. Duval.* In 1993, a Duval County School Board in Florida had a policy to allow a graduating class to have two minutes of uncensored speech for students to open or close graduation ceremonies. The ACLU sued for fear that the students could use this time for public prayer. The ACLU further stated that any students with backgrounds that indicated a tendency toward religious sentiment should not be allowed to speak at all at the graduation ceremonies. To add arrogance to lunacy, after the

11th Circuit Court of Appeals decided in the students' favor, Americans United for the Separation of Church and State published and distributed a pamphlet stating that schools should not count on this ruling because Americans United didn't agree with the ruling. Who on earth do they think they are? I am so tired of these leftist groups telling the rest of us that they will decide what our rights are, no matter what the Constitution, Congress or the courts say about it.

NON-CHRISTIAN FOUNDATIONS

Chinese civilization is more than four thousand years older than ours. Most modern European nations are centuries older than the United States. Yet we passed them all in freedom, power and wealth. I believe that a large part of the reason for this is that as we entered the modern industrial era, Christian influence declined in those countries that were once mainly Christian while it remained strong in the USA.

We did this by "melding Christian principles with civil government" as John Quincy Adams wrote. Note that he was not talking about a theocracy (liberal hysteria about the previous sentence can now cease.) Absolute civil power in the hands of anybody will corrupt them. This is why our founders wisely built in all those checks and balances: to minimize the power in one set of individuals.

One of the things overlooked by most people who idly stand by and watch our Christian foundation destroyed is that nature hates a vacuum. If this foundation is crushed and removed, some other group or philosophy will take over, and I guarantee you that it will be a far less freedom-granting "other."

"The reality today is that while we still have a choice, the choice is between a benign America, based on Judeo-Christian principles and on the other side is a very aggressive, sinister and power hungry secular fundamentalism that wishes to inject its tentacles into every single aspect of American life."[24]

---

24 Lapin, Rabbi Daniel as reported on the TV special "American Christian Heritage" broadcast on PAX TV on 4 Aug 2005.

To give an example of how it is in countries with other foundations: "Last year authorities jailed Pakistani Christian school teacher Pervez Masih, 33, on questionable blasphemy charges. Three teenage boys accused him of slandering the Muslim Prophet Mohammed in a private tutoring session. Under the blasphemy law, Pervez could receive the death penalty if convicted. He was denied bail and he remains in prison. At least seven other Christians are known to be in prison in Pakistan without bail on blasphemy charges, including one since 1996."[25]

Also in Pakistan, "Two Christian brothers await a final verdict after they were convicted of blasphemy for arguing with a Muslim vendor over ice cream bowls. Both were given 35-year prison terms, instead of the normal death sentences, for 'blasphemy against Islam and its prophet Muhammad' during an exchange with the ice cream man. Their appeal, expected before the Lahore High Court, has been on hold since June 1999."[26]

Another example: Notice in a church bulletin: "One of the Bible League's key ministry partners in India is in hiding, fearing violent treatment from *authorities* and Hindu extremists. Two other Christians associated with the Bible League have already been jailed. According to the All India Christian Council there is an attack against Christian workers or churches every 36 hours somewhere in India." (Emphasis mine.)

Notice that in these examples that it is not just extremists, but the governments themselves that persecute non-foundational belief systems—their foundations being other than Christian ones.

Abe Rosenthal was a journalist working for the *New York Times* when he decided to dedicate his life to using his talents and vocation to fight for human rights around the world.

After many years it was brought up to him that he was missing out on the largest violation of human rights in the world, the persecution of Christians. He, like everyone else in American society, had been constantly bombarded with the

---

25 Bandow, Doug "Slave Wages" *World Magazine* 4 May 2002: 22.
26 Belz, Mindy . "They Scream Over Ice Cream" *World Magazine* 29 June 2002: 7.

politically correct implication that Christians were always vic-
timizers, not victims. He was much more honest than most in
the major media, and in spite of his disbelief, he researched it.
He found out "about Sudanese believers who are sold into slavery by Muslims; of Pakistani Christians whose churches are
burned down by angry mobs; of Chinese pastors whose finger-
nails are pulled out because they preach the Gospel." He was
able to write five years of columns in his newspaper about
worldwide religious persecution.[27]

The reason I bring this up is that if you look at the facts, the
tens of thousand of Christians martyred every year, the thousands of lives saved by believers every year and the relatively
smaller amount of damage and greater good done by Christians
when compared to other groups, there is simply no logical reason to believe this notion that the world would be far better off
if there were no Christians. Yet that is the implication that the
liberal establishment has brainwashed us into feeling.

The examples above are from Muslim, Hindu and secular
cultures. Their foundations are different. In twelve of the original
thirteen American colonies the entire Ten Commandments were
incorporated into their civil and criminal laws.

BACK TO THE GOOD OL' USA

In a 1950 Florida Supreme Court Decision[28] it was stated: "A
people unschooled about the sovereignty of God, the Ten
Commandments, and the ethics of Jesus could never have evolved
the Bill of Rights, the Declaration of Independence, and the
Constitution. There is not one solitary fundamental principle of
our democratic policy that did not stem directly from the basic
moral concepts as embodied in the Decalogue." Yet the ACLU,
People for the American Way, People United for the Separation of
Church and State, etc., all sue to remove those very Ten
Commandments from our public buildings as yet another step in

---

27 Colson, Charles. "His Brother's Keeper: A. M. Rosenthal and Religious
   Persecution." Breakpoint Commentary #010712 7 Dec 2002.
28 *Florida v. City of Tampa*, 48 so.2d 78,79, 1950.

destroying those fundamental principles of our great country. When those principles are gone, so will be the country we loved.

Many people today don't think there is any good reason to go to church. But churches give a sense of community that is lacking in today's society. The missionaries and relief societies really do things that result in not only saving souls, but in saving thousands of lives worldwide every year. Somehow, I believe that the more people that go to church, the more cement is put back into America's crumbling foundation.

It is often overemphasized that there were individuals who were not Christians among our founding fathers. The groups that push this say that one of these was Benjamin Franklin. They use this as an implied assertion that these founding fathers would have gone right along with all the misuse of the "separation of church and state" to denigrate and abolish all public acknowledgement of any Biblical reference; yet, if we look at the record and listen to Franklin's own words, whether he was a Christian or not, he obviously didn't believe this nonsense.

When the constitutional convention was bogging down, Benjamin Franklin said: "God governs in the affairs of men. And if a sparrow cannot fall to the ground without His notice, is it probable that an empire can rise without his aid? We have been assured, Sir, in the Sacred Writings, 'except the Lord build the house, they labor in vain that build it.' I firmly believe this."

On June 26, 2002, judges of the federal Ninth Circuit Court of Appeals decided that it was unconstitutional for the Pledge of Allegiance to be recited in public schools, because of the words "under God." By inference this would mean that the Constitution rules out many other documents being read in schools such as: The Declaration of Independence ("Nature's God," "endowed by their Creator"), "God Bless America," George Washington's Farewell Address, minutes of the Constitutional Convention, and the Constitution ("in the year of our Lord" refers to Jesus.)

Add to this the fact that the Supreme Court of the United States begins each session with "God Save the United States and this honorable court," and that Congress starts out each day with the recitation of a prayer, and this ruling, and others like it, don't make any sense whatsoever!

You might ask: "Why should we care what their mindset or worldview was, or even what they really meant by what they said in the Constitution? After all, we are a modern society and are far more technologically advanced. They were, after all, just a relatively primitive culture." Glad you asked.

This is because people throughout all ages have the same characteristics. Details may vary from culture to culture and time to time, but people's propensities are alike throughout time. From the Emperor of Chin, centuries before Christ was born, to Adolph Hitler, we see that type again and again. There are misers, murderers, saints, thieves, people of integrity, liars, good, bad, ugly, and beautiful, the same throughout history. Just as there are individuals who devote their lives to the betterment of mankind, there are those who give just as much of themselves to enslaving mankind. Therefore, the wisdom of our founding fathers is as relevant today as the day the Constitution was written.

One of the main tenants of liberalism is the belief in the perfectibility of the human race. Unfortunately, a corollary of this, in their minds, is that this perfection can only be achieved in the absence of biblical Christianity. Cults are OK, other forms of religion are OK, for now, but those evangelicals and fundamentalists must be marginalized, their children indoctrinated out of their religion and, eventually, the sooner the better, Christianity will be moved into extinction. And, nationally speaking, they rip the foundation out from under their own house.

Since people are the same throughout history, we already know they, and we, are corruptible. The world has already tried socialism, feudalism, monarchy, dictatorship, parliamentarianism, anarchy, barter, money systems, non-monetary systems, civil rule, theocracy, atheistic rule, republicanism, democracy, ad infinitum. But we know that the government created by the worldview of our founding fathers created the freest, richest, most powerful nation that has ever existed on Earth. If we want to continue in that mold, we have to understand what gave this country its start and the principles that brought about all that

greatness. To throw away all that good for a newer way of thinking that might make things better, if people are perfectible, or at
least perfectly programmable, is the best example of complete
foolishness that I can think of.

WHY LIBERALS
HATE THE BIBLICAL GOD

Liberals' attempts to get God out of America started in
earnest over forty years ago. Madalyn Murray's victory in outlawing school prayer in the early 1960s came as a shock to most
Americans. For the first thirty years after this, these excommu-
nications of God from US culture through the courts and legislatures went unopposed because unlike the liberals, most
Americans did not understand why anyone would even want to
do this, nor do they understand how important this issue is.
Thus, nobody fought against this trend.

"Absolute power corrupts absolutely." Liberals understood
that no matter how powerful they became, as long as American
citizens are free and have so many rights, the power of the ruling
class is limited. Therefore, as they grew in power and increased in
their lust for more, they knew they must get rid of individual freedoms and rights in order to gain absolute power.

But the Declaration of Independence says: "We hold these
truths to be self-evident, that all men are created equal, that they
are endowed by their creator with certain unalienable rights,
that among these are life, liberty, and the pursuit of happiness."

Somehow liberals long ago correctly deduced that as long as
the biblical God was held in high esteem, He would be the highest authority. He is that creator from which we derive our rights.
If they could abolish God, then the government, not God, is who
gives us our rights. If government gives us our rights, government
can take them away. If government takes them away, the ruling
class usurps the power these freedoms once gave to the citizens.

The more God is censored, the closer you become to being
a helpless, powerless subject of the ruling liberal elite. Therefore,
I would suggest that we find out who is fighting on our side, for
our freedom, under God, and join them. (Some are listed in
Appendix One.)

A good example of how confused people can become without a sense of God can be seen in Princeton's teacher of Practical Ethics, Peter Singer, the "most influential" philosopher alive.

"He claims that his atheistic and culturally extreme views are the result of pure intellectual labor, but he acknowledges that he was 'impressed early on with my grandmother's argument: 'How could there be a God who would let the Holocaust happen?'"[29] Being Jewish and having relatives and friends with relatives who died in the Holocaust has had a part in his rejection of a biblical God.

Ironically, while looking at some of the things he teaches in his Practical Ethics class, I came to a startling realization. During his interview with Marvin Olasky, a series of questions and statements led me to a cumulative thought: "Is there anything wrong with a society in which children are bred for spare parts on a massive scale? 'No.' ..."He also reaffirmed that it would be ethically OK to kill 1-year-olds with physical and mental disabilities...." "...he favors legalized euthanasia for persons with Alzheimer's who cannot converse or recognize their children...." "He has consistently tossed aside the Declaration of Independence concept that all of us are created equal. Instead, the worth of a life varies according to its rationality and self-consciousness, with no essential divide between animals and humans." "He scorns attempts to set up standards of good and evil that go beyond utilitarianism, and hopes to convince people willingly to do it his way."[30] Suddenly the thought popped into my head: "Oh, dear Lord, he's teaching the ethics that led to the Holocaust."

ALL RELIGIONS ARE THE SAME

Leftists are in an awkward position with their philosophy that all religions are equal. If this is true, they have to support other religions than Christianity, which would include Islam as practiced in Iraq (under Saddam Hussein), Iran, and many

---

29 Olasky, Marvin. "Blue-State Philosopher" *World Magazine* 27 Nov 2004: 33.
30 Ibid; Pages 32-35.

other Muslim countries. That leaves leftists in "the uncomfortable position of having to demonstrate in support of a culture and an ideology that enslaves women, that kills homosexuals, rejects tolerance and forbids freedom."[31]

Many reading this chapter are still thinking: "Christian, Muslim, Hindu, et. al., all religions are the same." Lest you keep that conclusion, or should I say, liberal establishment propaganda programmed response, let us look at another specific example.

Eric Rudolph is a *self-proclaimed* Christian terrorist. The media loves to let us know he says he's a Christian. He is the bomber of the Olympics in Atlanta, several gay establishments, and some abortion clinics. In a letter to the editor in the *Arizona Republic*, Carl Goldberg of Tempe writes:[32] "O. Ricardo Pimentel's attempt Tuesday to set up an analogy between Christian and Muslim terrorism fails for the following reasons: (1) Eric Rudolph, the supposed "Christian terrorist," is pretty much a loner, whereas Muslim terrorists number in the many thousands; (2) Rudolph does not and cannot cite Christian scripture in support of his deeds, whereas Muslim terrorists continually cite passages from the Koran and other Islamic holy writings; (3) Rudolph has no support from Christian churches and clergy, whereas Muslim terrorists find continual support from Islamic religious authorities; (4) Rudolph receives no support from the larger Christian communities, whereas Muslim terrorists continue to enjoy widespread support, both active and passive, in the Muslim street and community organizations of many countries.

"Of course not all Muslims are terrorists; and, in the interest of justice as well as common sense, we must be very careful to distinguish those who support terrorists from those who do not.

"At the same time, we cannot afford to delude ourselves into believing that Muslim extremism is no different from Christian (or other religious) extremism.

"It is different and dangerously so."[33]

---

31 Veith, Gene Edward. "Culture" *World Magazine* 4 Jan 2003: 46.
32 Goldberg, Carl. "Muslim Terrorism different" *Arizona Republic* 11 June 2003: B10.
33 Ibid.

LOSING LIBERTY

"Religious freedom is under attack in the Western democracies—and in the name of human rights.

"At a time when Christians are murdered in the Middle East, imprisoned in China, and enslaved in northern Africa, it may seem strange to worry about freedom of religion in America and the West. Though American Christians are a long ways from being overtly persecuted, the right to the free exercise of religion is nevertheless being chiseled away. And though religious freedom has been considered foundational to all other rights, ironically, the new assaults on religious liberty are coming in the name of human rights.

"Outlawing religion can be done in two ways: by restricting what a religious group teaches or the way its followers live out their faith, or by requiring actions that go against a religion's teachings. Consider three cases:

(1) "Authorities in Sweden jailed a pastor for preaching that homosexuality is immoral and a violation of biblical teaching. He was arrested, tried, and sentenced to 30 days in prison for violating Sweden's law forbidding 'hate speech' against homosexuals.

"The Pentecostal pastor Ake Green is said to have forced the issue, announcing that he would break the law again, inviting authorities to hear his sermon, and sending them a tape when they did not show up. Still, the fact remains that a minister was arrested and imprisoned for preaching a sermon in his own church. Canada has passed a similar law, and gay activists are promoting hate-speech laws for the United States.

(2) "The California Supreme Court ruled in March that Catholic Charities must include contraceptive coverage in its health-insurance plans for employees, even though birth control violates Roman Catholic teachings. California law exempts churches from its contraceptive mandate, but the court ruled that a parachurch organization is not a church. The decision was upheld on appeal, but it now goes before the U.S. Supreme Court.

"Twenty other states have similar laws. Most include 'conscience clauses' exempting church bodies, but some do not. Wisconsin has no such law, but state attorney general Peg

Lautenschlager issued a ruling that mandates birth-control coverage anyway. Her ruling specifically includes the 'morning-after pill,' which induces abortion, and does not exempt churches and pro-life organizations. The attorney general's action will have the force of law if approved by a court.

"Meanwhile, pro-abortion groups are working to require insurance plans to cover abortions. NARAL and the ACLU are also trying to use the courts to force Catholic and other church-related hospitals to actually perform abortions, arguing that if they take federal funds they may not 'impose their religious beliefs' on patients who want to abort their children.

(3) "Organized efforts are underway to punish churches that become involved in conservative politics by taking away their tax-exempt status. In Kansas, the pro-gay-marriage Mainstream Coalition is sending teams to churches in an attempt to nail any pastor who preaches politics by turning him in to the IRS. Many churches are already under investigation, including those of Jerry Falwell and Ronnie Floyd, whose First Baptist of Springdale, Ark., is the biggest congregation in the state.

"The IRS code prohibiting churches from engaging in partisan political activity dates from 1954, when Sen. Lyndon Johnson inserted the provision in order to silence one of his critics. So far, it is being very selectively enforced. Democrats regularly use black churches for rallies and registration drives, to the point that candidates often give political speeches as the Sunday morning sermon. Only conservative churches are threatened for what a pastor might preach from the pulpit.

"What should Christians do to protect religious liberty? Legal threats have legal remedies. Hate-speech bills that criminalize moral judgments must be defeated. A bill called the Abortion Non-Discrimination Act would protect the right of hospitals, insurance companies, and other healthcare providers to refuse to commit abortion. It easily passed the House but is bottled up in the Senate. Passage depends on electing more Republican senators. A bill called the Safe Harbor for Churches Act would loosen restrictions on churches speaking up about politics, but it was killed in the House. Another bill, the Houses of Worship Free Speech Restoration Act, would remove the restrictions entirely.

"Protecting religious freedom will mean forming strategic alliances. Even Christians who have no problem with birth control should support the right of Roman Catholics not to be coerced into violating their own teachings. Even Christians whose theology rejects the preaching of politics from the pulpit should support the right of other churches to preach whatever they want. And notice how much protecting religious freedom will hinge on the next election."[34]

In conclusion I would simply state that it is obvious that our country does have a Christian foundation and we must preserve it to maintain our greatness.

---

34 Veith, Gene Edward. "Losing Liberty." *World Magazine* 4 Sept. 2004: 29.
Reprinted by permission from *World Magazine*, Asheville, NC.

Chapter 4

Homosexual Agenda

This is an unfortunate chapter to have to write, because I, like most Americans, have a live and let live attitude. It goes against my grain to interfere with other people. But it has become obvious that I didn't start this controversy, and it will not only affect my life, but help to bring about the end of America if we all say nothing and just let others gain control of our children's and grandchildren's lives.

In 1972 the major homosexual/lesbian organizations in the US got together to decide what exactly was their agenda. It would come to be called the 1972 Gay Rights Platform. (This meeting might be compared to the Republicans and Democrats having conventions to decide their political platforms.)

Some of the planks of the platform wouldn't bother most people; they don't bother me. Some of them are laughable, such as the demand "prohibiting discrimination in the federal civil service because of sexual orientation, in hiring and promoting." I once worked in a civil service department of about forty-five employees, about one-third of which were gay, and two of the supervisors were gay. But at least three of these planks would cause most people to see three red flags pop up. Most of the non-offensive ones could be summed up by the example: If a man works as a plumber for ten years, doesn't bother anybody, and one day it is found out he is a homosexual, he shouldn't be fired just for that. No big deal, who cares? It's none of our business.

But several items that should bother most people are not so innocent. Three of these are: (1) Legalization of homosexual marriage, with adoption rights; (2) A homosexual hired in every public school in America, grades kindergarten to 12, for the express purpose of teaching a class that brainwashes our children and grandchildren into believing that homosexual sex and lifestyle are equal in all ways to heterosexuality; and (3) the complete abolition of all age-of-consent laws.

It doesn't take a rocket scientist to figure out that if an authority figure (a teacher in a public school) tells kids for years before puberty that the one lifestyle is just as legitimate as the other, many will be turned in that direction that otherwise would not have; especially if they can reach them before or during that very natural stage where they reject members of the opposite sex. (If they didn't go through that stage, sex would probably start even younger than it does now, and it is a well known fact that on average, the younger you start having sex, the more probable it is that it will damage your life.) If the homosexual teacher can reach them at this stage, he/she can convince some of them that these feelings mean they must be homosexual. Then if they can get age-of-consent laws repealed as "Archaic Laws," the teacher has a whole classroom of potential sex partners, or one-half a classroom, if he/she can just get them to say "yes."

If the way they have gotten their way in other countries is any indication, they will do the implementation of their platform, or agenda, incrementally. They usually have gotten age-of-consent laws "modernized" by shaving off two or three years at a time. In Great Britain they got the age changed from 21 to 18 at first. A couple years later they got it changed again to 16. As of this writing, they were most successful in the Netherlands (Holland), getting the age of consent lowered to 14. (Supplemental note: Since I originally researched this book, Spain has surpassed Holland with lowering the age of consent to 13. And since I wrote this last sentence, the Netherlands, Spain and Portugal have lowered the age of consent to 12.)

Most people don't even understand the attitude of this lobby. It can be summed up in two rules:

1) Everybody must be made to do everything our way all the time.
2) Every compromise is only temporary until rule #1 is achieved.

Most people in real life, or day-to-day living, have to make compromises. When they do, they figure they got half of what they wanted and they let the other guy have half of what he wanted. But the homosexual lobby has already gotten way beyond their half. Their stated objective is not just to be accepted and allowed to live and let live, but to force everyone to condone, admire and proselytize their way of life. And they want us to give them our children and grandchildren as well.

I think that to understand this chapter you really need to know exactly what the 1972 Gay Rights Platform says. Keep in mind that the words "sexual orientation" include the orientation toward adult-to-child sex (state #7 below) and group marriage (state #8). Perhaps, in the future, it will even be made to include group sex and human-to-animal sex. Oh, sorry. Group sex is already covered in state #8.

The 1972 Gay Rights Platform
FEDERAL

1) Amend all federal Civil Rights Acts, other legislation and government controls to prohibit discrimination in employment, housing, public accommodations and public services. (1972 Federal-1)
2) Issuance by the President of an executive order prohibiting the military from excluding for reasons of their sexual

orientation, persons who of their own volition desire
entrance into the Armed Services; and from issuing less-
than-fully-honorable discharges for homosexuality; and
the upgrading to fully honorable all such discharges previously issued, with retroactive benefits. (1972 Federal-2)

3) Issuance by the President of an executive order prohibiting discrimination in the federal civil service
because of sexual orientation, in hiring and promoting;
and prohibiting discriminations against homosexuals in
security clearances. (1972 Federal-3)

4) Elimination of tax inequities victimizing single persons
and same-sex couples. (1972 Federal-4)

5) Elimination of bars to the entry, immigration and natu-
ralization of homosexual aliens. (1972 Federal-5)

6) Federal encouragement and support for sex education
courses, prepared and taught by gay women and men,
presenting homosexuality as a valid, healthy preference
and lifestyle as a viable alternative to heterosexuality.
(1972 Federal-6)

7) Appropriate executive orders, regulations and legislation banning the compiling, maintenance and dissemi-
nation of information on an individual's sexual
preferences, behavior, and social and political activities
for dossiers and data banks. (1972 Federal-7)

8) Federal funding of aid programs of gay men's and
women's organizations designed to alleviate the problems encountered by gay women and men which are
engendered by an oppressive sexist society. (1972
Federal-8)

9) Immediate release of all gay women and men now
incarcerated in detention centers, prisons and mental
institutions because of sexual offense charges relating to
victimless crimes or sexual orientation; and that adequate compensation be made for the physical and mental duress encountered; and that all existing records
relating to the incarceration be immediately expunged.
(1972 Federal-9)

STATE

1) All federal legislation and programs enumerated in Demands 1, 6, 7, 8, and 9 above should be implemented at the State level where applicable. (1972 State-1)
2) Repeal of all State laws prohibiting private sexual acts involving consenting persons; equalization for homosexuals and heterosexuals for the enforcement of all laws. (1972 State-2)
3) Repeal all state laws prohibiting solicitation for private voluntary sexual liaisons; and laws prohibiting prostitution, both male and female. (1972 State-3)
4) Enactment of legislation prohibiting insurance companies and any other state-regulated enterprises from discriminating because of sexual orientation, in insurance and in bonding or any other prerequisite to employment or control of one's personal demesne. (1972 State-4)
5) Enactment of legislation so that child custody, adoption, visitation rights, foster parenting, and the like shall not be denied because of sexual orientation or marital status. (1972 State-5)
6) Repeal of all state laws prohibiting transvestism and cross-dressing. (1972 State-6)
7) Repeal of all laws governing the age of sexual consent. (1972 State-7)
8) Repeal of all legislative provisions that restrict the sex or number of persons entering into a marriage unit; and the extension of legal benefits to all persons who cohabit regardless of sex or numbers. (1972 State-8)

Gays used to ridicule anyone who even hinted that they were "after the children." Up until I read the 1972 Gay Rights platform, in the year 2000, I fell for that, just like most people. I had had no idea that their stated objective was that they were indeed after the children (Federal demands #6 & 9; State demand # 2, 5 & 7 above). Of course, there is that inconvenient statistic that although homosexuals are only about 3 percent of the population (at this time), they are 35 percent of the child molesters. Unfortunately, unless you get involved and vote pro-homosexual agenda politicians out of office, the agenda will continue going forward until it is 100 percent accomplished. Think about Federal Demand #9, which is also incorporated into State Demand #1: "Immediate release of all gay women and men now incarcerated in…prisons and mental institutions because of sexual offense charges relating to…sexual orientation" (which includes orientation toward children, as is made obvious in State Demand #7: "Repeal of all laws governing the age of sexual consent") "…adequate compensation be made for…mental duress encountered; and that all existing records…be immediately expunged."

After having become more familiar with what the homosexual agenda is really about, and how they have no intention of permanent compromise, I look at the homosexual lobby as analogous to the Grimm's fairy tale "The Emperor's New Clothes."

To refresh your memory, in the story a couple of con men come to the capital city of the empire and convince the Emperor that they make the most fabulous clothes in the world—but they are magic clothes and the stupid and ignorant cannot see them. They then "make" him a "new suit," but, of course, there is really nothing there. But nobody wants to admit that they are stupid and ignorant, so they praise the clothes lavishly and the emperor winds up in a big parade displaying his new wardrobe. Everybody has been informed that stupid people cannot see them, so everybody praises the outfit, not wanting others to find out how stupid they are. Finally, a young innocent child says, "But he has nothing on." Then everybody realizes he is right and the Potentate is thoroughly embarrassed and everybody laughs as the procession moves on.

Likewise, we have been thoroughly brainwashed with the "modern" view that homosexuality is normal, a legitimate alternative lifestyle and people are just born that way. If people are just born that way, why are they trying so hard to recruit the children? Some day some innocent is going to say, "These are people with serious psychological problems that participate in unnatural sex acts." And, hopefully, we will all come out of our

hypnotic state and say, "By golly, he's right." And I hope this realization becomes common knowledge again before it is too late
and they take over the next generation.

WHAT IF?

Let's extrapolate. Suppose two hundred years ago everybody
became exclusively homosexual. Today the human race would be
extinct. And although there are those who don't think of this as
a bad thing, most of us would disagree. For those who would
counter with the other extreme: Suppose two hundred years ago
everybody became 100 percent promiscuously heterosexual. By
now the twenty-some-odd sexually transmitted diseases that
have reached epidemic proportions would have decimated
humanity, the world economy would be endemically depressed
and AIDS would be in the process of wiping out the human race.

Just for fun, let's take "all things in moderation" to the
extreme. Suppose all people on Earth practiced abstinence until
marriage, practiced monogamous marriage "'til (natural) death
do us part" and didn't practice sex outside of marriage for the
last two hundred years. Virtually every sexually transmitted disease would be extinct. No one would ever have heard of AIDS.
No women and children would be under the poverty line due to
desertion by the father of the children, no men would be sleeping on a friend's couch due to child support payments. The subject of abortion wouldn't be controversial since the need for it
would almost certainly never have arisen in the first place. The
emotional horrors and situational disasters in peoples' lives that
have exploded with the results of the 1960s sexual revolution
would be vanishingly rare. (The sexual revolution is one of
those few wars in which both sides lost.)

TOLERANCE

Time after time you have heard the phrase, "People must be
tolerant," in regard to homosexual activism. Once again, I am
not referring to the individual homosexual. Just like someone
who has manic depression or paranoia or schizophrenia has a
disorder, I want them well. I don't want them harmed because

they have extra problems or just because they are different. So it is with homosexuality. Would you want a "paranoid-schizophrenia lobby" to get a member placed in every public school, grades kindergarten through 12, teaching the children that everybody is out to get them and they can't trust anybody and that this is just a legitimate, alternative way of looking at things?

Referring to the Gay Lesbian Straight Education Network (GLSEN), a *Washington Times* article stated: "Its goals 'extend to...holding diversity seminars for teachers and students and ensuring that only positive discussions about homosexuality are allowed into elementary school classrooms, including kindergarten,' according to the GLSEN Web site."[35]

But I am talking about tolerance of the homosexual *agenda*. May I suggest that tolerance of pure evil is stupid? You wouldn't "tolerate" a fire burning down your house, you'd fight the fire; you would stop the destruction if you could. The gay "fire" (agenda) is one of the four main "fires" that is burning down our country. I will be called "homophobic." Well then, I will confess to other phobias as well. I'm bestial phobic, pedophilia phobic and sadomasochistic phobic as well. By these standards, I'm all screwed up. But I do not believe that most Americans have these standards. I must note here that once again the left is changing the language. "Phobia" means fear. I, and most Americans, do not fear gays. The vast, overwhelming, majority of people that the proponents of the gay agenda would call "homophobic" are not, because they oppose the gay agenda on moral and practical grounds, not out of fear. Some oppose it simply because they understand that there will be dire consequences to institutionalizing government sanctioning of a sexual deviance and trying to spread it with the full force of the government behind it.

Most Americans have been extremely tolerant of the gay agenda in the past. But we must realize that homosexuals will not tolerate anyone being allowed to disagree with their agenda, any part of it, including the abolition of all age-of-consent laws, which will legalize pedophilia (child molestation.)

---

35 *The Washington Times*. 3 July 2004: A4. As reported in *The Journal* Oct. 2004: 6.

Keep in mind that if you truly believe that your sexual orientation is genetic, you don't recruit. If homosexual propagandizing/brainwashing through the school system is implemented and works, and I believe that if it infiltrates our schools it will work, then the percentage of the population that is homosexual will grow. Come to think of it, if being gay were genetic, can you think of any gene less likely to get passed on to the next generation than homosexuality? If homosexuals really believed that they are just born that way, why would they spend unimaginable time, effort, energy and money trying to recruit our young people into their lifestyle? I would recommend that we quit listening to people who obviously do not themselves believe what they are saying. Ironically, if the infiltration of our schools does lead to a burgeoning of the gay population, it will prove beyond a shadow of a doubt that sexual orientation is not genetic. After all, a white person does not bother trying to "recruit" a black person to become white, or visa versa.

If all public schools are turned into gay sex mills, I predict that the gay percentage will go up, doubling every ten to twelve years. If in the year 2000 they were 3 percent, then by 2012 they will be 6 percent; by 2024, 12 percent, by 2036, 24 percent.

To show how demanding some gays can be, take the example of Ellen Degeneres. When she was asked why she moved from Hollywood to the Santa Barbara area she said that it was because Hollywood is too anti-gay. That's like someone saying that Hugh Hefner is too much of a prude.

To stop this slide into the abyss, a lot more average Americans have to get involved. "The hottest places in Hell are reserved for those who, in a period of moral crisis, maintain their neutrality." — Dante.

It is possible that with the homosexualization of one or more of the state school systems in the first years of the new millennium, by the time this is published, we may have started seeing the results of just a couple of years of this madness.

If a large number of kids have been "converted" to gayness, all kinds of statistics will prove what I have been saying. The problems that may occur with straights and gays together in the

showers at schools could become so severe that physical education classes and intramural sports may have to be cancelled.
Then watch the obesity problem escalate as well. Before I even
started writing this book, many teachers had already been programmed to call innocent children who do not totally agree
with the homosexual agenda "homophobes," which is causing
more problems in the heterosexual kid's psyche. But these
"teachers" do not care about doing damage to kids with politically incorrect ideas. They are expendable.

The homosexual lobby has done a brilliant job of propagan-
dizing everything portrayed about it in the media. Outlined in
an article in a gay magazine called *Guide* in an article entitled
"The Overhauling of Straight America," the authors, Kirk and
Pill state: "In the early stages of any campaign to reach straight
America, the masses should not be shocked and repelled by premature exposure to homosexual behavior itself. Instead, the
imagery of sex should be downplayed and gay rights should be
reduced to an abstract social question as much as possible. First
let the camel get his nose inside the tent—only later his unsightly
derriere!"

"Gays must be cast as victims…straights will be inclined by
reflex to assume the role of protector…we intend to make the
anti-gays look so nasty that average Americans will want to dis-
associate themselves from such types." The complete psychiatric, public relations and marketing strategy is fleshed out in
the book *After the Ball* by Marshall Kirk and Hunter Madsen,
copyright 1989.

As you can see, this preplanned strategy has worked wonderfully well. We have fallen for the "I was just born this way,
I'm a helpless victim; won't you be my hero by protecting me
and my civil rights" act, hook, line, and sinker. First they got
virtually complete acceptance by society. In some states, in the
near future, the legislators may turn over indoctrinating all the
kids in the public schools into homosexuality to the homosexuals. Next will come the abolition of all age-of-consent laws.
The only way to start reversing this takeover is to vote against
pro-gay agenda politicians and ask your congressman to

impeach judges who legislate the gay agenda from the bench. Once again, I EMPHASIZE, these people have a sexual deviancy, we want to help them get well, if and when they want such help. If they don't want such help and don't hurt anybody, leave them alone. We don't want to hurt them. But we do not want to help them spread their problems to the next generation with government assistance. At the very least, we want them to quit trying to legislate their immorality and stop trying to take away the freedoms and rights of non-gay Americans. (For reasons I do not totally understand, in countries where most of the gay agenda has been implemented, including gay marriage, those countries have lost freedom of speech, freedom of the press, freedom of religion and freedom to peaceably assemble. If you express your moral or religious or secular opinion that there is something not normal about homosexuality, you can be arrested, fined and/or spend time in prison. In other words, gay marriage would somehow have the effect of repealing the First Amendment to the Constitution. Gay marriage is now legal in Belgium, the Netherlands, Spain, and Canada. Civil unions, sometimes called de-facto gay marriage, are the law of the land in Sweden, Denmark, France, Germany, Finland and Norway.)

METHODS OF ATTACK

The new millennium has brought an increased ferocity from homosexual and other liberal groups wishing to squash any and all opinions that differ from their own. At the University of North Carolina the Intervarsity Christian Fellowship (IVCF) was ordered to change its fifty-two-year-old charter or lose its official recognition and any student organization funding. The charter states that membership in the IVCF is open to everybody, but the group's leaders must be Christians. The University demanded that the leadership be open to all. After a threatened lawsuit, the University decided to relent and leave things the way they have been for fifty-two years.[36]

---

36 Plowman, Edward E. "Brought to Heel" *World Magazine* 18 Jan 2003: Pg. 9.

"Homosexual activists have taken aim at evangelical groups on campuses across the country, accusing them of discrimination and pressuring administrators to compel compliance."[37]

The obvious ploy here is either force the Christian organizations off campus or out of existence, OR force them to accept homosexuals in leadership positions, overwhelm the membership with gays, vote all gay leaders in, and turn the club into yet another government sanctioned homosexual "evangelical" arm. Once again, the only way to counter this clever plan is for many more Christians and others who understand the dangers of the "homosexualization of America" to join such organizations and participate fully. This is where the gays usually win. Gays are unbelievably well-organized and unlike most other groups of people, a vastly superior percentage of homosexuals are politically active. To give a hypothetical example: University X has 30,000 students. There are 10,000 Christians on campus of varying degrees of religious commitment. There are 900 homosexuals. The campus Christian organization has 500 members. The university forces them to accept anybody in leadership positions. 600 homosexuals join, vote as a block for the new leaders, all homosexuals are voted in and all semblance of Christian mission disappears from the group forever. And the club still has a respected religious name giving the less-than-well-informed people around campus the impression that those with a biblical worldview have now come to embrace homosexuality. The plan is near perfect, and as long as politically incorrect people don't get involved, this plan will work every time. The other 9,500 Christian students could easily join and out-vote the gay splinter group. But they are working hard to get their degrees, they are having fun, they don't want to get involved and they don't need another thing to do. We all feel overwhelmed, we understand. But if we don't get involved, those who wish to destroy everything good in our society for their own perceived personal gain will always win and eventually they will be the only ones in America who have any freedom left.

---

37 Ibid.

WHAT YOU CAN DO

Now that this (and other) radical agenda(s) have been systematically introduced, they can only be stopped by much higher participation of the non-homosexuals and non-leftists that remain. In other words, only you can stop the madness.

If a company advertises on a gay show, find out about it, verify it (even if you have to watch the offensive show once) and stop buying that product! Then write the company and tell them this and why you are doing it. If you're like me, the product will probably be one of your favorite things. But your children and grandchildren are literally at stake.

If a specific network or cable TV channel does a pro-gay show or series, do not watch that channel for the rest of the season. Cancel that cable channel. Let them know about what you are doing and why. I know that that channel has some of your favorite shows, some of the best shows. But what you may not have come to understand is that if a gay show is not watched, but other shows on that network are, the advertising profits from the highly rated shows are now being used to keep the gay show on the air. It is the same with movie studios. To be totally effective, if you want to go the extra mile, you need to boycott all the movies in a given year by a studio that produces any gay propaganda films (or other offending films), not just the bad films, or the profits from the nice films will ensure that the bad films are produced.

ARE WE BRAINWASHED?

By 2002 the homosexual lobby had declared all out war on anyone who does not 100 percent support their agenda. The other side (most Americans) lost the first many battles simply because they were lulled to sleep and did not know they had been attacked. Imagine waking up to a newspaper headline informing you that you've been asleep for twenty years (like Rip Van Winkle) and that New York, all of New England, Florida, Hawaii and California are now occupied by a foreign power. I would suggest that it might be time to do something about it. This analogy is closer to reality than most US citizens realize.

People have been brainwashed into thinking that it is the homophobes (anyone who is not 100 percent in favor of the homosexual agenda, including legalization of pedophilia) who have serious mental problems.

If you think I am exaggerating by using the term "brain-washed," I want you to take a test right now. See if I can "read your mind" by asking you what your gut reaction is to certain words: Christian Coalition; the rich; Jerry Falwell; fundamentalists; National Rifle Association; homophobes; conservatives; pro-lifers. Somewhere in there, did you have negative gut reactions? Look away from this page for five seconds if you need to think about it.

Now comes the mind reading part: "Well, I would have had a negative gut reaction if you had said Nazi or neo-Nazi." If I just quoted or paraphrased what you were really thinking, then your programming is complete; you just regurgitated what you've been told to think. Think about it: I wrote this months or years before you read it and just now I read your mind. Do you really think it's a coincidence? Hopefully, this paragraph applies to only a small percentage of the people who read it.

The entire liberal establishment: the government bureaucracy, most educational institutions and the mainstream media have been saturating us with the leftist point of view for decades. You need to—some for the first time—find out what the other side believes. A good start would be to contact the Christian Coalition (CC) and ask to be sent their voter guides. These short, informative pamphlets will explain how the CC stands on certain issues and then quickly lists how your Senators and Congressmen have voted on those issues, which is often just the opposite of how they told their constituents they would vote on those issues. Even if you oppose everything the CC stands for, they give you the information to vote against their point of view. But if you agree with them, you had better get out and vote against those who support everything you are against.

MOVING ON

It was interesting to watch how the media handled the Catholic Church's priests-molesting-boys story. The liberal media was in a total dilemma. The church was usually fairly conservative on most subjects, so the general media relished a story that would put it down. But they realized that the problem was not with church policy, but with the fact that the American church had allowed the hiring of homosexuals as priests for the last few decades, which is actually against church policy. Since any liberal is totally in favor of hiring gays in any and all positions, they had to make it look like a non-gay issue. They bent over backwards to spotlight the scandalization of the church without mentioning anything about homosexual perpetrators. By scouring the nation they finally came up with a few stories of priests having molested girls. But if you look past the propaganda, you had to realize that it was a gay problem. More than 90 percent of the time, the victim was a boy.

It seems silly to me, but I realize that I must define a certain word before I use it. We have been programmed to think that discrimination means racism or bigotry. And it can mean that. But generally to discriminate simply means to make choices based on your considered opinion. When you are single, you discriminate when you make a judgment that you would rather go out with one person than another. If you are a confirmed non-discriminator you must pick your dates randomly, with no forethought as to common interests, looks, personality, et al. It is the same with a surgeon. You discriminate when you require that someone who operates on you must have a medical degree. Thus, when the Boy Scouts fought to ban homosexuals from being leaders, they did discriminate and were perfectly just in doing so. The Catholic priesthood in America did not do so and look what happened.

In the 1972 Gay Rights Platform, one of the goals is the abolition of all age-of-consent laws. Thereafter, any grade-school child could consent to having sex with an adult and there would be nothing anyone could do about it. The vast majority of Americans does not agree with this, and find it quite reprehensible. As the Catholic homosexual priest scandal proves, homosexuals should not be put in positions where they are alone and in charge of children. Places that find gayness immoral should not be forced to hire gays. Places like churches, day care centers, Boy Scout troops, Christian business owners. You don't force someone to hire a known embezzler or a schizophrenic and put them in charge of accounts receivable or some complex situation that will aggravate their condition. Why would you put people who push for the abolition of all age-of-consent laws in charge of children?

Also, it is easy to deduce that the First Amendment of the Constitution guarantees, under the freedom of religion clause, that if your religion considers homosexuality a sin, you do not have to hire gays. This is a sticky subject though. As a representative of the church, by being an employee, you almost definitely would not hire them. But what if you own a print shop and they are a qualified worker? As a Bible- or Koran-believing person, you feel being gay is sin. But you yourself are a sinner, and so are all your employees. How do you know that God hasn't put this applicant there so that you can lead them out of this particular sin? It is a dilemma that each individual will have to deal with themselves. The Constitution makes sure that the right to make that decision will not be taken away from you. But courts and legislators have been ignoring the parts of the Constitution that they do not agree with lately.

In the 1990s we treated the sexual deviancy of homosexuality like it was an endangered species, precious and in need of protection. But in the new century we are no longer trying to preserve it, but have turned to aggressively trying to spread it.

It's as if a group of mad scientists in 1918 decided that the flu epidemic that killed over 20,000,000 people worldwide was a good thing and even more people should get the disease.

A CASE IN POINT

There was an article published in *World Magazine* that was so perfect in showing what we might be looking forward to, so macabre and foreboding, that I had to ask permission to reprint it here.[38]

---

38 Veith, Gene Edward. "Sweden's Shame" *World Magazine* 10 Aug 2002: 12.
   Reprinted with permission, *World Magazine*; Copyright 2002,
   www.worldmag.com.

"Culture Beat: Liberal Sweden, supposedly a land of tolerance, is about to make criticism of homosexuality a crime.

"Sweden is the liberal utopia. Confiscatory taxes fund a cradle-to-grave welfare state, with 'free' health care, job security, and government regulation for all. Sexual freedom is taken for granted, to the point that the *majority* of Swedish couples live together without being married, and the *majority* of children are born out of wedlock.

"Sweden has become so tolerant that it is taking the next step: prosecuting those whom it considers intolerant, even if this means throwing out freedom of speech and freedom of religion. The Swedish parliament has passed a constitutional amendment that would make it a crime to teach that homosexual behavior is immoral.

"The Swedish constitution affirms freedom of expression but makes exceptions. 'Freedom of expression and freedom of information may be restricted,' says the constitution, under certain circumstances, including speech that would 'imply the unfavorable treatment of a citizen because he belongs to a minority group by reason of race, color, or ethnic origin' (Chapter 2, Articles 13 & 15). The amendment, which must be approved by one more vote after the new parliament convenes in September, adds 'sexual orientation' to that list of groups that must not be subject to 'unfavorable' speech.

"Sweden's Criminal Code already has laws against 'insulting' or 'agitating against' minorities. The constitutional amendment, if approved, would go into effect in January, effectively outlawing the teaching that homosexuality is morally wrong. A pastor, for example, who teaches what the Bible says about homosexual sin could go to prison for up to four years.

"Despite—or perhaps because of—the Swedish culture's hostility to Christianity, that country has a vibrant Christian community. Remnants of the hopelessly liberal state church—abolished in 2000—remain, but as many as one-third of the pastors in the Lutheran Church of Sweden are conservative. There are also many independent churches—Lutheran, Pietist, Baptist, Pentecostal—as well as Roman Catholics and

Orthodox. Swedish evangelicals are known throughout Europe for their evangelistic zeal, particularly in sending missionaries to the former Communist states.

"The new law would presumably outlaw the use of the Roman Catholic catechism—which teaches that homosexuality is a sin—as well as the teachings of Islam. (Sweden's ultra-tolerant immigration policies have brought in some 300,000 Muslims.) As Swedish Christians understand the law, they would be allowed to quote the Scriptures, but they would not be allowed to say that what the Scriptures teach on the matter is applicable today. If they do, they could go to prison.

"The new law is only one front in the Swedish establishment's war against Christianity and other conservative religions. Conservative pastors and Christian schools report constant harassment by government officials.

"Indeed, parental rights—like other 'family values'—have gone the way of the Viking ships. Spanking one's child is a criminal offense. The government tells children to turn in their parents if they attempt to punish them. The government has taken away children from Christian parents on trumped-up child-abuse charges, because of even mild exercises of physical discipline.

"Organizations ranging from Amnesty International to the United Nations oppose human-rights abuses, and the United States regularly slaps sanctions on nations that violate human rights.

"Persecution of Christians around the world has gained new attention. China, Sudan, Iran, Indonesia, and other Muslim and African nations have been the most noted offenders, and have received widespread condemnation for their anti-Christian oppression. But will white, European, progressive Sweden face the same kind of sanctions and international condemnation if they start imprisoning people for disapproving of homosexuality? Sweden is a member of the European Union, whose founding documents commit member nations to human rights and to policies of religious tolerance. Will the EU discipline Sweden if it amends its constitution to allow religious persecution?

"Will the United States lodge a statement of concern or of protest, through the State Department or the American Consulate or a resolution from Congress, to discourage the new parliament from ratifying the new law? We do that sort of thing to Israel, when it mistreats Palestinians, and to Serbia, when it mistreats its religious minorities. When the offenses are particularly flagrant, we cut off trade against the oppressive nation. Should we not give Sweden the same treatment?

"More importantly, is Sweden just slightly ahead of where the United States will be in a few years? Will anti-discrimination laws, which punish external actions, develop into laws that punish inner convictions and beliefs? Will the desire to be tolerant mutate into an oppressive intolerance against intolerance?"[39]

Most Americans believe that a person should not be arrested, tried, convicted of a crime and thrown into prison for having politically incorrect beliefs. Yet that is exactly what will happen if the homosexual agenda is not stopped and reversed.

Human nature being what it is, your first reaction may be: "I don't want to get involved. I'm no hero. I just want to keep quiet and live my life in peace." That attitude is what is allowing the left wing Orwellian society to be so near completion. If you do not get involved, once the takeover is complete, you will live the rest of your life in fear. Will you accidentally say something that annoys the liberal establishment? Will your child tell the school you said something about not wanting them to become gay? Will you spend years in prison, lose your job and your pension because of a slip of the tongue? Living a life where you have to fear your own thoughts will make life not worth living.

BIAS IN THE MEDIA

In 1998 Matthew Shepard was viscously murdered. It was thought that he was a homosexual at a bar late at night trying to pick up on two guys whom he did not realize were not only straight, but very dangerous people. These former convicted felons played along and they all left the bar together intent on having a night of "fun."

---

39 Veith, Gene Edward. "Sweden's Shame" *World Magazine* 10 Aug 2002: 12.

It was further reported that, unfortunately for Matt, their idea of fun was very different from his. He was looking forward to homosexual activities; they were intent on torturing and murdering "the queer." Upon revelation of the incident, the media went into a frenzy. In the single month after Shepard's murder, there were over three thousand stories in the major media. It was a horrible occurrence and I believe that both of the men who did this deserve the death penalty.

On September 26, 1999 Jesse Dirkhising was murdered. Jesse was a thirteen-year-old boy who had been enticed into doing homosexual acts by two homosexuals who lived in his neighborhood. But this time it turned out differently. He was sodomized (homosexually raped) by them, tortured, and murdered. (Although, the death was the result of sloppy S&M sex, the participants did not actually intend to kill Jess. If he was over eighteen, then it would be manslaughter.) In the month after Jesse's murder, there were 46 stories in the media about this. There were none on CNN, ABC, NBC and CBS at that time. "It was a horrible occurrence and I believe that both of the men who did this deserve the death penalty."[40] In both cases life in prison was given to the murderers.

The men who murdered Matt were total social misfits. Their records show criminal behavior, prison time, etc.

The men who murdered Jesse were simply described as "drifters."

Even after the "underground" media, more conservative sources, not readily available to the general public, complained about the obvious bias in the treatment of the two stories, to my knowledge, only Peter Jennings of ABC had the guts to do a story on the possibility of bias on the two stories. True, his conclusion was still that there was no bias, but the other major media sources would not even allow a dissenting opinion to be heard.

Just to give a further example of the pro-homosexual bias of the media, look at the case of Mary Stachowics. She was a woman who confronted a nineteen-year-old gay man with her

---

40 See above paragraph.

belief that homosexuality is wrong. He killed her and hid her body in a crawl space under his living quarters. This was five years after the Matthew Shepard murder. A Lexis/Nexis search showed that that month Mary got five news stories. Matthew got, that month, five years after his death, 47 news stories.

The vast majority of the times, especially in the fictional media, homosexuals have to be portrayed as the hero, the nice guys, or the victims. They are rarely the victimizer, the bad person, the evil anti-hero. Even in movies based on a true story, if the bad people are homosexuals, the true story part is not mentioned. The movie *By the Numbers* with Sandra Bullock was based on the famous murder case of Loeb and Leopold, the two being homosexuals in the 1930s who killed people for the thrill of it. (The movie was updated to take place in modern times.) It was not specifically mentioned that the bad guys in the movie were homosexuals.

MATTHEW SHEPARD UPDATE

On November 26, 2004 ABC aired a 20/20 episode that exposed the fact that the entire Matthew Shepard murder was about drugs and money. It was a robbery. The murderer, Aaron Mckinney, was on methamphetamines and went into a drug-induced frenzy; beating, torturing and murdering Matthew. Matthew being used as a poster boy for gay rights was based on false testimony of people who thought, in some twisted way, that the sentence for Aaron would be lighter if the jury thought that Matt had made unwanted sexual advances to Aaron. But, by the time this testimony was given, the media had already convicted all of America of a hate crime against gays.

"Hate-crimes laws are a centerpiece of the homosexual movement's attempt to suppress dissent and normalize homosexuality…

"Shepard's death led NBC's Katie Couric to insinuate that groups including the Family Research Council and Focus on the Family were indirectly responsible for his murder 'by having an ad campaign saying, "If you're a homosexual, you can change your orientation." That prompts people to say, "If I meet someone who is homosexual, I'm going to take action and try to convince them or try to harm them."' Following the ABC investigation, Focus on the Family asked NBC…for an official apology for that remark…. NBC responded by refusing to apologize."[41]

ARE THE PEOPLE HEARD?
THEY WILL BE IF THEY PERSIST.

Somehow the way the media portrays gays brainwashes us into the acceptance of homosexuality and even moves us to pass laws to protect an abhorrent, perverted and degrading lifestyle. Further, we make laws to punish those who believe that sodomy, rimming and other same-sex acts are not normal, and should not be encouraged.

In the California State Legislature, the first gay caucus has been formed. One of its first acts was to push for a bill that would give same-sex partners equal rights with married couples. This was after the voters overwhelmingly passed Proposition 22 in 2000, prohibiting state recognition of same sex marriages. "The irony: The caucus's official status entitles it to a part-time legislative staffer. That means the same citizens who voted to ban same-sex marriage are now paying to support a group bent on subverting their will."[42]

In March of 2000 California voted on a referendum that was brought before the citizens. It stated: "A spouse in a civil union shall have all the same rights, protections, benefits, and responsibilities under law…that are granted a spouse in a civil marriage." It was voted down by the citizens two to one. Ignoring this, the California state legislature in 2002 brought the same language as the referendum in a bill that would have superseded the will of the people (AB 1338). This bill, if passed, would have forced all people, businesses and churches, etc., to treat homosexual unions as marriages. There were "no exemptions for

---

41 Unnamed author. "Shepard murder wasn't hate crime after all." Focus on The Family Citizen, Feb 2005: 9.
42 Vincent, Lynn. "Left-coast libertines" *World Magazine* 8 Feb 2003: 26.

churches or religious organizations."[43] Anyone not complying with the law could be fined $150,000. Also this bill would have required schoolchildren to participate in pro-homosexual activities like "diversity" assemblies and "gay days" or face disciplinary action. Further, it would have given a spouse who divorces to enter a "civil union" equal (if not greater) consideration in child custody decisions than the innocent heterosexual spouse who remains unmarried. The law was heavily lobbied against by what are called pro-family groups and it was defeated. But it will be re-introduced both in California and other states.

Think about this. When such a law is passed, any nonprofit organization that does not agree to pay benefits to unmarried people living together can be fined out of business. Churches (including the Salvation Army), food banks, homeless shelters, relief agencies and others who refuse on moral grounds to pay out, will be fined, in many cases, out of business. Freedom of religious belief will be outlawed and punishable by law and fine. But they say that this does not violate the First Amendment of the Constitution!

One of the unintended (?) consequences of such laws will be a tremendous rollback in benefits paid to married couples. Many small businesses and nonprofit organizations struggle financially anyway. Some cannot afford to pay the extra benefits. But they will only have to pay them if they pay them to married couples. So they will stop paying benefits (health insurance, life insurance, pension survivor benefit) to married couples as well. This in turn will devastate families financially. For example, instead of paying $100 per month for health insurance through the company, you will have to pay over $400 per month for a policy from a private company, or go without.

These homosexual legislative agenda items will start a huge trend of punishing anyone who disagrees with any part of the homosexual agenda. The rest of us will no longer be free in the truest sense of the term.

---

43 Sears, Alan. *Alliance Defense Fund Newsletter*(s) Apr/Jun 2002: 2, 3.

LATE, BUT NOT TOO LATE

Across the nation, rules and laws are being passed to force everyone to accept, approve and actually fund homosexual behavior. On college campuses, student tuition, even from those opposed to condoning homosexual behavior, has been used to fund the campus gay/lesbian clubs. In high schools and even grade schools, public money is used to promote the homosexual lifestyle as a legitimate alternative to heterosexuality.

Even the fact that people are seriously proposing laws to promote the gay lifestyle and punish those who disagree with it means we who do disagree have waited too long to take action. We have passed the initial stage for action. Some such laws are already on the books. If we wait any longer to take action or say something, it will be illegal to do or say anything when the liberal establishment starts the process of turning our own children against everything we believe in. And we will be punished, fined and/or jailed for saying or doing anything politically incorrect (whether on this subject or on any other.)

SCHOOL DAZE

In bygone days, public schools could have teachers that read from the Bible or from individual preacher's sermons. People, teacher or student, could pray with no consequences, and God and the Ten Commandments were not yet banned.

Now that much of this has been censored, we find that it did leave a vacuum. The National Education Association (NEA) has proposed that this vacuum should be filled with teaching the kids about homosexuality and how good it is. After that recommendation, why does anyone who is not a homosexual belong to the NEA? I know that there are other teacher unions. I would think that there must be a non-politically correct alternative to such things.

The *Massachusetts News* ran a story in March of 2002 about an all-day seminar at Tufts University sponsored by the Massachusetts Department of Education on how to force homosexual "education" into the public schools. The government cannot sponsor a religion, but it can sponsor events that will lead to teaching our children the wonders of perverted sex?

And speaking of those all important things that government needs to meddle in: Many municipalities are now removing any Boy Scout organizations from the United Way donations list if those Boy Scout groups refuse to give up their constitutional right to not accept gay leaders over the boys. Since when was it government's job to harass people who exercise their constitutionally guaranteed rights?

THE MAN (OR WOMAN) ON THE STREET

Does the average homosexual on the street aim to destroy the USA? I don't think so. As a matter of fact, I hope the rank and file gay person does not agree with their leadership's goals. Less than 18 percent of all adult gays have had a relationship that lasted as long as three years. Why would the gay on the street be gung ho on gay marriage? Most gays do not molest children. Why would they, as a group, be totally behind abolition of all age of consent laws?

I think most gay people have not thought through or extrapolated the consequences of their leaders' ever-strengthening political agenda. We must not hate the individual homosexual anymore than we hate someone because they suffer from depression, or any other mental or physical ailment, or even a vastly different point of view. Nevertheless, we need to stop and reverse the advance of the homosexual *agenda* for the protection of our beloved America.

PERPETUAL POWER

To get you to understand the danger of the homosexual lobby, consider how dangerous most people perceive these groups: the Ku Klux Klan; the skinheads, the Hell's Angels; the Bloods, the Crips. To the extent that some of the members of some of these groups have tried to "take over," they have been limited by people's wariness of them. Now consider that homosexuals vastly outnumber all these groups combined and they have the power of the liberal establishment completely behind their power grab. The educational branch of our society is helping them force homosexuality on even our grade school children. Gays are always portrayed as the good guys in the media, and anyone who does not agree with the entire homosexual agenda is either, evil, stupid, or both. In politics, legislation to empower the homosexual lobby is passed somewhere in this country every year.

This all leads to the vicious circle of your tax dollars going to gay organizations, which then grow and use that growth to influence the various levels of government to give them still more money.[44]

In 2002 the Lesbian and Gay Men's Community Center of San Diego had income of $2.8 million. Seventy percent of this money was government money. This is how your elected representatives put your tax dollars to work. A politically correct person would say: "Thank God they didn't give it to a Bible-believing church!"

Hillcrest Youth Center in San Diego is "a tax-funded drop-in program for homeless and disaffected kids who are 'lesbian, gay, bisexual, transgendered or questioning.'" It received almost $2.0 million from government agencies.[45]

New York State gave over $500,000 to similar gay groups. Since 1990 the number of gay centers that cater to young people has increased tenfold, more and more of the financing being given by federal or local government agencies. I really doubt that the majority of American voters intended that part of their money go to encourage young people to join the gay lifestyle. Think of it, part of your property taxes, part of your income taxes, part of your sales taxes is devoted to making as many of the youngest generation homosexual as is possible. Even without quibbling about sexual mores, the waste of government money is appalling.

---

44 Vincent, Lynn. "Leading them into temptation" *World Magazine* 15 Jun 2002: 42 & 43.
45 Ibid.

BEGINNINGS

"The American Psychiatric Association, under political pressure from a vitriolic internal gay caucus, ignored...science and removed homosexuality from its list of disorders in 1973. But science just wouldn't go away: Researchers have since found causal links between homosexuality and a lack of male role models (*Journal of Genetics and Psychology*, 1983); parental emotional abandonment (*Journal of Psychoanalysis*, 1989); and child sexual abuse (*Child Abuse and Neglect*, 1992)."[46]

"A 2001 study in the *Archives of Sexual Behavior* compared childhood molestation between heterosexuals and non-heterosexuals. The authors found that almost half of gay men and about one in five lesbians reported homosexual molestation in childhood. This compared to childhood homosexual molestation rates of only 7 percent of heterosexual men and 1 percent of heterosexual women."[47]

When the American Psychiatric Association (APA) took homosexuality off its list of disorders in 1973, it had the effect of legitimizing gay sex and the gay lifestyle. The APA based its decision on two main things: A report by Evelyn Hooker and the actions of Judd Marmor, a high ranking official of the APA.

"Evelyn Hooker...published a scientifically bogus paper that supposedly showed no differences in the psychopathology of homosexual and heterosexual males. In the late '60s she chaired a task force that excluded anyone who believed that there was anything in the least problematic with homosexuality—meaning that she excluded the entire body of clinicians who until then had devoted their careers to the subject. She similarly ensured that all its mental-health members were collaborators of Alfred Kinsey."[48]

Even though the Kinsey report had already been discredited as invalid, it was used to set policy recommendations "claiming that homosexuality had been shown to be normal, a degree of bisexuality was the universal norm....

---

46 Ibid.
47 Ibid.
48 Marvin Olasky, "From Mental Disorder to Civil-Rights Cause" *World Magazine*, Feb. 19, 2005: 30.

"Judd Marmor was on his way to the vice presidency of the American Psychiatric Association. He and a number of allies in the APA arranged to have outside gay activists disrupt APA meetings to protest the persistence of homosexuality as a diagnostic category within their list of disorders."[49] Research was conducted leading to the removal of homosexuality from the APA's list of disorders. "...the 'research' consisted largely of Hooker's bogus work and Kinsey's data."[50] Remember that unlike the film that portrays Kinsey as "a mild-mannered scientist who just naively stumbles into this kind of work," in real life he was "a real pervert who had an agenda.... Kinsey's legacy includes, among other things, the modern school sex-education movement, the myth that 10 percent of Americans are gay—and according to the Centers for Disease Control and Prevention, a population in which more than 30 percent of people over 18 have an incurable sexually transmitted disease...."[51] Kinsey also had a "role in the brutal molestation of hundreds of children."[52]

Where did Kinsey get the idea that only 6 percent of Americans are exclusively heterosexual?

Maybe we should look at what he used as a sampling of "average" Americans: "For example, 25 percent of the people he interviewed for his study were prisoners. Another 5 percent were male prostitutes. And 100 percent were people who volunteered to talk about their sex lives, something most people in the late 1940s and 1950s would be reticent about doing. In other words, Kinsey employed no sampling to ensure that his data accurately reflected the population.

"Most disturbing is Kinsey's study of the sexual activity of children, *as young as 2 months old*. The descriptions of trying to bring them to a state of sexual release can only be child abuse."[53]

---

49 Ibid.

50 Ibid.

51 Hamrick, Kristi "Ministry's position on film draws media spotlight" *Focus on the Family Citizen*, Feb. 2005: 6.

52 Ibid.

53 Gene Edward Veith. "Outing a fraud" *World Magazine* 18 Dec 2004: 22.

The APA is an association of professionals like any other. They have some expertise, but in the subjective realm of the mind, do they have some kind of power to decree to you and me what is normal and what isn't? What if the AMA decreed that syphilis was no longer a physical disease? Would that make you think there was no harm in having sex with a person who had syphilis? NO. You would use your own judgment and decide that no matter what the AMA said, syphilis is still a disease and you would avoid contamination.

Similarly, no matter what the APA says, for the sake of all the children at risk, you had better start thinking about what gay lifestyles are practicing and whether you really believe that this is sexual deviance, or any one of a number of other categories. The politically correct establishment, believe it or not, cannot take away your right to decide that some things are abnormal. Although, soon, they do plan to take away your rights to declare that you believe this is abnormal.

MORE RECENTLY

Ted Kennedy has proposed what they have titled the "Local Law Enforcement Enhancement Act." Paradoxically, it would allow *federal* police agencies to declare that any act perpetrated against a homosexual could be declared a hate crime, and therefore, punishable by more severe penalties than a similar crime against, say, a woman, a child, or the elderly. This bill is one of many legislative moves across the country to make those who participate in a sexually deviant lifestyle a specially protected class of citizen. Most people, even after decades of brainwashing techniques being used on them to accept homosexuality, still see it for what it is—aberrant behavior. Yet the government continues to protect and promote it.

In Canada these types of laws are already the law of the land. People there have already been fined thousands of dollars for simply publishing Bible verses that said that homosexuality was wrong! Freedom of speech and religion are now merely history in Canada. Do we really want to give them up here too? Just to be politically correct? Just to be nice to a well-organized group of sexually deviant people who are doing everything they can to enslave our children and take away our freedoms? I really doubt it.

"I've said several times on the air that the Judeo-Christian value system in Canada, our neighbor to the north, is on the ropes, literally. As a case in point, on September 6 [2002], a court actually declared any law defining marriage as an exclusive union between one man and one woman as unconstitutional and discriminatory.[54] Is this where we are headed in the United States? Yes, unless we awaken to our peril."[55]

GAY MARRIAGE

Gay marriage is an experiment of very recent origin. No society that I know of prior to modern times has even tried it. But fortunately for the United States of America, four countries have enforced it recently. We don't have to try it to find out the *immediate* consequences.

In the Netherlands, Belgium and Canada, gay marriage was implemented. Immediately, for all practical purposes, freedom of religion and freedom of speech and freedom of the press were outlawed.

"For example, in Canada, Bill C-250, which now makes it a criminal offense to publicly express 'hatred' (read: *moral disapproval*) against people who engage in homosexual behavior, has become law. The extremists want to import these laws from Canada into our legal system."[56]

"Whoever would overthrow the liberty of a nation must begin by subduing the freedom of speech." —Benjamin Franklin

As 2003 passed and 2004 started, The Massachusetts Supreme Court as a result of its decision in *Goodrich vs. The Massachusetts Department of Health* unconstitutionally ordered their legislature to pass legislation making gay marriage legal. A couple of municipalities started issuing gay marriage licenses illegally in other parts of the country. If you had access to more than one source of news, it seems like not a day passes that the media isn't pushing

---

54 2 CP. "Quebec Gays Hail Court Ruling" *Toronto Star* 7 Sept. 2002: A9.

55 Dobson, Dr. James. "Family News from Dr. James Dobson" Oct. 2002: 6.

56 Sears, Alan E. "Tomorrow Is Here" *ADF Briefing* July 2004: 4.

the story on us. We have been backed up against a wall to the point where it seems we have only two choices: (1) Allow gay marriage and rescind the first amendment to the Constitution (all five parts of it) or, (2) Pass a Federal Marriage Amendment to the Constitution, defining marriage as exclusively between a man and a woman. Number (2) will only happen if you call your congressman and senators and encourage them, politely, to support this. A cute aside to the debate over passing the Federal Marriage Amendment is the radio commercials one hears that "Conservatives will be against the Federal Marriage Amendment." The commercial is paid for by the Human Rights Campaign, one of the leading gay rights advocating organizations. I doubt if anyone considers it one of the top conservative think tanks.

Keep in mind that we do not have to repeat this social experiment to know the immediate consequences. Gay marriage is already legal in the Netherlands. On average these gay marriages last one and a half years and the "married" gay participants average eight sex partners outside the committed relationship while they are "married."[57] Obviously, marriage does not mean the same thing to gay couples that it means to heterosexual partners.

Let us further realize that marriages create families, by adoption, the traditional way, or some variations of both that have become more popular since the '60s. What have we learned about the healthiest families in the past forty years?

"'...on average, children do best when raised by their two married biological parents.'[58] *Child Trends* also recently observed that, 'An extensive body of research tells us that children do best when they grow up with both biological parents.'[59]

---

57 Munsil, Len. "In support of the Federal Marriage Amendment" Family Voice Talking Points Feb 2004

58 Parks, Mary. "Are Married Parents Really Better for Children?" *Center for Law and Social Policy, Policy Brief,* May 2003, Pg.1, as reported by Glenn T. Stanton in "What About the Kids?' In *Focus On the Family Citizen,* Oct. 2004, Pg. 27.)

59 Moore, Kristin Anderson, et al. "Marriage From A Child's Perspective: How Does Family Structure Affect Children, and What Can We Do about It?" *Child Trends Research Brief,* June 2002, Pg. 1, as reported by Glenn T. Stanton in "What About the Kids?" in *Focus On the Family Citizen* Oct. 2004, Pg. 27.

"A wise and compassionate society always comes to the aid of children in fatherless and stepfamilies, but a wise and compassionate society never, never intentionally subjects children to such families. But every single same-sex home would do exactly that and for no other reason than that a tiny minority of adults desires such families."[60]

One last note before I close: Isn't it interesting that the 1972 Gay Rights Platform does not demand a declaration that homosexuality is not a mental disorder. Yet the APA did not remove homosexuality from its list of mental disorders until 1973. Sort of sounds like they knew that is was already a done deal, doesn't it? Since around half of that platform is already accomplished, I wonder if the rest of it is already a done deal even now, if the average American does nothing and just lets it slide.

In our rush to give everyone as much freedom as possible, we have forgotten that by its nature if you give evil enough freedom, it will turn right around and take away yours.

---

60 Ibid.

Chapter 5

1960s Foolishness

M any mantras from the sixties are still popular and being spread by the liberal establishment today in spite of the fact that if we just think about them, they are absolute foolishness.

1) SEX IS JUST GOOD, CLEAN FUN AND HAS NO CONSEQUENCES

One of the most significant results of the 1960s sexual revolution is that it made much of the next generation of young men into a subculture of sexual predators. Conveniently, it made many of the next generation of young women into willing victims.

The practical consequences of sex outside of marriage has been an increase in women being used and abused, more single women raising children, more women having abortions that leave them emotionally scarred in addition to the scars left from one sexually bonded relationship broken after another. And then there is the sexually transmitted disease epidemic.

From *The Journal* May 2002 page 7, published by American Christian College, Colorado: Referring to a 2001 Department of Health & Human Services report entitled 'Scientific Evidence on Condom Effectiveness for Sexually Transmitted Disease Prevention: "The report first gave the numbers of new cases of STD's in the year: 63,000 new cases of HIV/AIDS, 70,000 of syphilis, 650,000 of gonorrhea, 1 million of genital herpes, 3 million of chlamydia, 5 million of trichomoniasis, 5.5 million of human papillomavirus."

The article continues: "Thus, according to our own government, condoms are a fraud. And partly because they believe that fraud, 45 million Americans now suffer from herpes, for which there is no known cure, and 900,000 suffer from HIV/AIDS."

To help this sink in, let's turn to an article by Andree Seu: "My high school days in the '60s seem Edenic by contrast. We knew only of simple gonorrhea and syphilis (a shot of penicillin would make you right as rain), and only one out of 32 of your classmates had an STD. In 1983 it jumped to one in 18; in 1996, to one in four. And with over 30 new STDs today, 30 percent of them incurable, that's a lot of polysyllables to know.....

"But knowing is a political business in this world. Meg Meeker, in *Epidemic: How Teen Sex is Killing Our Kids*, writes that one in five Americans over the age of 12 has genital herpes. (Reread that statistic and let it hit you.)" "'...a lot of teachers and physicians are intimidated by Hollywood and by businesses which seem to have taken over our kids and are selling sex,' Dr. Meeker says. This from a woman who used to hand out Depo-Provera like Altoids at her women's college until she started seeing kids come back to her office with cervical cancer and herpes."[61]

Dr. James Dobson, in an interview on Fox News' *Hannity and Colmes* said: "The federal government has spent $3 billion in the 30 years to promote the safe sex ideology, and it's been a disaster. At the time they started, there were only two sexually transmitted diseases that were at an epidemic level, and there are now

---

61 Seu, Andree "In The Know," *World Magazine*, 12 June 2004: 71.

more than 20. One in three Americans over 10 years of age has a sexually transmitted disease.'"[62]

I would add to Dr. Dobson's criticism of the "safe sex" program that when it started the USA had a 6 percent birth out of wedlock rate. After 30 years of "safe sex" we have a 30 percent out of wedlock birth rate. Why do we still have these programs when they have had the opposite effect of what they promised?

The failed sexual revolution also increases hunger and poverty in the USA, in a way that need never have existed.

More women and children live under the poverty level today than did in the 1950s, mainly because of having children in, or out, of wedlock and being deserted by the men responsible. For example: The good news is that the number of families in poverty, from 1959 to 2001 went down from 8.3 million to 6.8 million. The bad news is that the number of families headed by women that were in poverty went up, from 1.9 million to 3.4million.[63]

As long as women or girls are willing to accept one meaningless relationship after another, then that is what they will get by giving in to the pressure to start having sex to keep the relationship going. For those who do not like to think in moral terms, that is OK too. The practical benefits of abstinence before marriage far outstrip moral considerations in the secular mind if you will just look at the statistics and think about it.

So keep in mind that if you are a woman and are having sex outside of marriage, you are working against your own best interests on several levels. Actually, when you think about it, this statement is true of men too.

2) GAY IS OK

As you saw in the chapter on the gay rights movement, this is not a harmless individual choice, nor is it genetically predetermined. But for reasons most of us will never understand, the political force that has evolved has become one of the most dangerous to the continued existence of America. Some element of

---

62 Buchanan, Patrick J., *Human Events*, 11 March 2002: 14.
63 U.S. Census Bureau, Historical Poverty Table #13.

exaggeration in the leaders' minds has led them to believe they need not only freedom, but to crush all opposing points of view, destroy those who would not hand over their children and grand-children for indoctrination and solicitation. Admittedly, this is one thing that could not have been predicted. But now we know.

3) MONEY DOES NOT MATTER

Mostly 1960s flower power types were spoiled kids of an increasingly affluent middle class. We had all the modern toys— neat cars, eight tracks, stereos, color TVs, etc., and had not worked for any of it.

We were attending a college with a hefty allowance so we could have all the fun, as well as opportunities that our parents could not have during the Depression and WWII. In retrospect one person of the WWII generation said (paraphrasing): "We tried to make it better for the next generation, but made it worse…We gave too much without making them earn it. As a result, they have become less self-reliant."

Thinking that money did not matter, the way a person who just ate a Thanksgiving dinner might think food does not mat-ter, many of us didn't prepare for our financial futures. Then, once on our own, when real life hit us like a bus, we went over-board and became more materialistic than the previous genera-tion that we had condemned for being too materialistic.

Money matters. You can do great good with it for yourself, your kids and others. Love of money can be as addictive as drugs, but a healthy respect for it is a good thing to have. (See Appendix 2 for Rules for Success for Young People.)

Another problem caused by having so much without paying for it is the abuse of credit buying. Wanting everything now, we just charged it. Those credit cards and loans eventually come due, even if one does not seem to be aware of this fact.

4) DRUGS ARE COOL

Wrong. I saw someone I cared about get hooked when he was sixteen. He was bright, handsome and personable when he was young—the type that people thought had a future. Once drugs got hold of him, all that mattered was the next fix. Now he is in his mid-forties, has had a string of broken marriages and other relationships that ended. He has no job, no education and no friends, spends lots of time in prison, and only owns the clothes on his back.

When he was in his mid to late twenties, he came into a legally acquired lump sum of money equal to paying cash for a 1300 square foot house. Within six months, he had blown it all, mostly on drugs. Supplemental note: Last week his mother called me to let me know that he lost a job he needed to fix his rotting teeth, went back on drugs and his body couldn't take them anymore. He died at age forty-five.

Two others I have known that had "innocent" flirtations with drugs did not do very well either.

These two guys destroyed the function of small organs in their heads with illegal drug usage. Now they have to take prescription drugs to replace the chemicals those structures secreted or they cannot even think straight. The damage is permanent. They have been off illegal drugs for years, but they can never go off the prescription drugs they will always need to replace those natural chemicals.

5) YOU CAN'T LEGISLATE MORALITY

One of the buzz phrases that became popular in the sixties that is still being used by the left to lull us into inaction is, "You can't legislate morality." If we were paying attention we might have noticed that in the real world the phrase should have morphed to: "If you don't legislate your morality, someone else will legislate theirs." More recently this evolved into, "If you don't legislate your morality, someone else will legislate their immorality."

People have been led down a path that makes them no longer realize that all legislation (law) is based on one person's morality or someone else's morality. In 2004 John Kerry ran for president. On the subject of abortion, he stated that he personally believes that abortion is wrong, but he had not voted in the Senate to impose his convictions on others. This sounds kind of noble, very sixties, but when you think about it you realize that he then voted to impose someone else's morality on everyone, voting for positions that he believes are wrong. A true leader votes his convictions and if his constituents don't agree with him, they vote him out of office. And if he voted his convictions, he can accept that.

If you truly believe that you cannot legislate morality, then you do not believe in making any laws at all. To say that one person should not take from another without compensation (stealing) is a moral judgment. To say that a person should not settle his grievance against another person by harming or even killing that person is a moral judgment. Deleting moral guidelines leads to immorality, which leads to anarchy, which leads to chaos, which is quickly replaced by a dictatorship (or a warlord system) or the takeover of your country by another country.

Dr. Martin Luther King said: "Morality cannot be legislated, but behavior can be regulated. Judicial decrees may not change the heart, but they can restrain the heartless."

6) YOU'LL TURN YOUR KIDS OFF TO RELIGION

"Don't force your kids to go to church or they will grow up hating it."

According to a nationwide poll by researcher George Barna, the probabilities of people accepting Jesus as Savior are, by age: five through thirteen: 32 percent; fourteen through eighteen: 4 percent; nineteen and above: 6 percent. It seems pretty obvious that not teaching your children when they are young, and then expecting them to magically accept whatever religion or philosophy you hope they will when they are older is nonsense.

7) THE OPPOSITE OF LOVE IS NOT HATE, BUT INDIFFERENCE

You hardly have to think about this one to disprove it.

It's 2:00 A.M. in a bad part of a major city. You get off the freeway on the wrong exit, make a bad turn, and pass a group of young, dangerous looking men who give you bad looks because you are of a different group than they are (known by the way you dress and/or the nice new car you drive and/or race, etc). Just before you passed them, you passed an all-night gas station, now two blocks away; you run out of gas. You take your gallon gas can and have to walk back past these guys to get gas. If you don't want them to "opposite of love" you, by the standards of the title of this subsection, you would rather they hate you than be indifferent to you. I think most of us would rather they be indifferent to us; but not a 1960s philosopher. Hate is less bad than indifference.

When you hear about all the suicide bombers and think of the horrible terrorist acts going on around the world, you realize that most of these maniacs have been taught to hate from the time they were little. This is unbelievably sad. But I guarantee you that every victim of these hate-filled people would rather they had been indifferent. The opposite of love is not indifference, it IS hate.

8) SEX IS GOOD FOR FRIENDSHIPS

Even the Seinfeld show wound up admitting that sex between friends (Jerry and Elaine) can ruin a friendship. Then they had the friendship go on anyway, but that was necessary for the show to continue. In real life I would guess that over 90 percent of the people who have tried mixing sex with friendship have found out that it does not work. One person, no matter how hard they try not to, will bond with the other. But the other won't. It happens like that most of the time. Then it has to end, and you get hurt badly. And, to tell you the truth, sexually transmitted diseases don't care whether you are romantically involved or not, they still transmit during intercourse.

MARRIAGE IS JUST A PIECE OF PAPER. ALL YOU REALLY NEED IS LOVE!

Though Stanley Kurtz' article in the *Weekly Standard* is mostly about how gay marriage has contributed to the death of heterosexual marriage in countries that already have de facto gay marriage, it contains facts of relevance to marriage in general.[64]

---

64 Kurtz, Stanley. "The End of Marriage in Scandinavia" *The Weekly Standard* 2 Feb 04.

People will argue that divorce rates have gone down in countries where people just living together are the norm. Obviously, if you don't get married, there is no record of when you split up. "...cohabiting couples with children break up at two to three times the rate of married parents."[65] Kurtz goes on to explain how the increase in dissolution of families (couples with children, whether married or not) has made it necessary to expand the welfare state to the point where there is no choice but for virtually all women to work just to pay the enormous taxes. Thus the children are turned over to the state for programming; I mean, "raising."

Liberals are often saying that they are doing things "for the children." If this is true, then let us encourage marriage instead of cohabitation, get rid of no-fault divorce, and make it harder to leave your spouse, since the vast majority of studies prove beyond any shadow of a doubt that, on the average, couples splitting up is bad for the children.

IN CONCLUSION

These and many other influences from the rebellious 1960s still control the liberal agenda. It's like they never outgrew adolescence. Free love, legalization of drugs, vilifying of Christians, conservatives, big business, capitalism, traditional American culture, and lack of patriotism are always at the center of the liberal agenda. These things were all at the center of the 1960s' counterculture. Maturity has led most Americans to realize that these things are wrong. So let's stop electing liberal politicians whose strongest ambition is to lead us in the wrong direction.

---

65 Ibid.

Chapter 6

The Oligarchy
of the Judiciary

In 1969 Red Skelton said: "I pledge allegiance to the flag, of the United States of America, and to the Republic for which it stands, one nation, indivisible, with liberty and justice for all. Since I was a small boy, two states have been added to our country, and two words have been added to the Pledge of Allegiance, 'under God.' Wouldn't it be a pity if someone said that is a prayer and that would be eliminated from schools, too?"

When Red Skelton said this in 1969, he was referring to the tragedy of the 1962 court ruling that outlawed prayer in public schools after more than 150 years of Americans taking school prayer as a "for granted" given. When he said this, it was sobering, but no one seriously thought his scenario would come to pass. But on June 26, 2002, the US Ninth Circuit Court of Appeals in San Francisco ruled the Pledge of Allegiance as unconstitutional, due to the inclusion of "under God." Thank you, Judge Alfred Goodwin and Judge Stephen Reinhardt, for knowing so much better than the vast majority of American citizens.

Ironically, if this ruling stands, it will ban the reading of many other documents in the public school, two of which are rather interesting. This ruling would make it unconstitutional to read in public schools: (1) The Declaration of Independence ("laws of…Nature's God," "…endowed by their Creator,") and (2) The Constitution of the United States of America (Article VII "…in the year of our Lord," which refers specifically to Jesus Christ, thus according to this ruling is a government establishment of the Christian religion.)

Please listen carefully to the following! Federal judges are appointed for life by the president, but must be confirmed in the Senate. Most Americans do not like the liberal activism of the leftist judges that form the majority of the Feds. Most people realize that for the last forty or more years, the judges have started legislating from the bench as well as usurping the executive branch's veto power of legislation. Thus they have been siphoning power both from the legislative branch and the executive branch of the government, upsetting the balance of power. Further, traditionally, unless they have committed some crime or have shown malfeasance, a president's candidate for the federal bench has been confirmed by the Senate without any problem, senators figuring that liberal, conservative and moderate numbers will eventually balance. But since the day Reagan left office, this practice has been abandoned by the liberal politicians in the Senate. Yes, when the Senate was more conservative in the 1990s, 86 percent of Bill Clinton's liberal appointments were confirmed the first two years he was in office. But when George W. Bush became president and the Senate was ruled by the liberals, only 43 percent of his were confirmed in the same time span. Virtually none of his more conservative judges were even brought up to a vote for confirmation. Even once the Republicans regained the majority in the Senate: (1) liberal Republicans voted with the Democrats and (2) the Democratic minority started using tactics, including filibuster, to stop conservative nominations. Senator John Kerry, the year he ran for president, gave the example: he said he is "prepared to filibuster, if necessary, any Supreme Court nominee who would turn back the clock on a woman's right to choose."

In 2003 it was reported that the Senate had confirmed only 53 percent of Bush's appeal-court nominees compared to over 90 percent of Presidents Clinton, Bush I, and Reagan. "And in March, Democrats deployed a parliamentary weapon never before used by a partisan minority to kill a president's judicial appoint- ments: They launched filibusters to block full-Senate votes on two Bush nominees...."[66]

"For the first time in American history, a minority of senators is using the filibuster...to replace majority rule with minority rule...That is, a minority seeks to defeat judicial nominations the majority would otherwise approve."[67]

Since conservative-leaning Presidents tend to balance the number of right-leaning judges with a similar number of left- leaning people, but liberal presidents almost always nominate leftist, activist judges, the court system has been stacked with far left, anti-constitutional, activist judges.

Now comes the most important part of this! If you do not like the bizarre way the court system is dismantling your free- doms and unilaterally repealing your rights under the Constitution, YOU MUST STOP ELECTING LIBERAL POLITI- CIANS. They have found out that by letting the courts usurp their power, if they appoint these leftist judges, the judges will install the entire left-wing agenda for them! And if anybody notices the slow erosion of their freedoms, the senators who confirmed the judges can say, "Don't look at me, I didn't vote for any legislation that caused this." Let me restate this differ- ently. A certain liberal senator will emphatically denounce the rulings of a leftist activist judge, and then turn right around and confirm another judge that he knows will make the same rulings. (Hint: the senator is lying when he acts dismayed at the liberal activist judge's rulings.) That same senator will help block a strict constructionist, conservative judge that will not read into the Constitution a leftist agenda.

---

66 Vincent, Lynn. Tyranny Of The Minority *World Magazine* 7 June 2003: 16–17.
67 Concerned Women for America legal analyst Tom Jipping as reported in the previous footnote.

Understand that they will take away all your freedoms without voting them away and suffering your wrath at the voting booth, by simply confirming the appointed leftist judges to do it for them; this, and rejecting judges that believe that the Constitution means what it says, no more, no less. I cannot overemphasize this. Please stop voting to give up your own freedoms by electing liberal politicians. They seem to want to give away lots of goodies, so you will re-elect them. But I will guarantee you that whatever you get will not be worth the price of freedom.[68]

THE TEN COMMANDMENTS

In May of 2002, the ACLU won a case where US District Judge Allan Edgar ordered the Ten Commandments plaques removed from Hamilton County courthouses (in Tennessee) because they violated the constitutional separation of church and state. What Judge Edgar obviously does not know is that the Constitution never mentions separation of church and state. He too has been brainwashed to believe that it is in there somewhere. You would think that by the time a person becomes a federal judge he would have been required to read the Constitution at some point during his schooling! He stated: "Experience tells us that there is perhaps nothing more divisive than the interjection of religion into our government." A spokesperson for the ACLU said that this was "a victory for religious freedom." (How's that for redefining "victory"?)

In Alabama Judge Myron Thompson ordered the Ten Commandments out of the entry of the Alabama State Judicial Building, deciding that they are unconstitutional endorsements of religion. Consider these two decisions and then realize that there are two renditions of the Ten Commandments in the United States Supreme Court Building in Washington DC. That would make these two federal judges either woefully ignorant or completely irrational. Either way I would recommend that everyone reading this call their congressman and ask that these

---

68 For a more complete look at judges' usurping of power, see the book: *Coercing Virtue: The Worldwide Rule of Judges*, by Robert Bork.

two be impeached for malfeasance due to these rulings. Unless we start using impeachment again, we are "voting" for the end of rule of law and the complete subjection, by us, to the oligarchy of the judiciary.

What would the founding fathers think about a judge ordering the Ten Commandments being removed from a courthouse? Maybe it can be inferred from what they said. For instance: James Madison, Father of the Constitution and architect of the first amendment said: "We have staked the whole future of American civilization, not upon the power of government, far from it. We have staked the future of all of our political institutions upon the capacity of mankind for self-government; upon the capacity of each and all of us to govern ourselves, to control ourselves, to sustain ourselves, according to the Ten Commandments of God."[69]

BROADER ISSUES

Before we can understand how out of control the federal judiciary has become, we need a few examples of blatant discrimination by the judges when they have got to know they are violating the intents of the founders to restructure our society in their own image:

1) "Despite the public, governmental prayers offered by the authors of the First Amendment, and despite the decision of the First Congress (that approved the First Amendment) to pay for Bibles to be printed and distributed in public schools, the courts have ruled that prayer and Bible reading in public schools are unconstitutional.

2) "Despite the clear teaching of our nation's founding document, the Declaration of Independence, that the 'right to life' is a core principle of our nation, and despite the teaching of the Constitution that life cannot be taken without due process of law, the courts have

---

69 As reported by: Munsil, Len *Family Facts* 26 Aug 2003, 1.

declared abortion to be a fundamental constitutional right.

3) "Despite the presence of two renditions of the Ten Commandments in the United States Supreme Court building and courtroom in Washington D.C., a federal judge has ruled that Alabama's display of a Ten Commandments' monument violates the First Amendment.

4) "Despite consistent reference to and reliances upon Almighty God in the public laws and constitutions of our nation and of every state, one federal court has declared the phrase 'under God' from our Pledge of Allegiance to be unconstitutional."[70]

5) Despite the fact that five million California voters voted in favor of Proposition 187, which would have prohibited giving taxpayer benefits to illegal aliens, one federal judge, Mariana Pfaelzer, nullified it after it passed.

Terence P. Jeffrey wrote about how the Congress that drafted the first amendment also hired the first congressional chaplain; how they petitioned George Washington to recommend a day of public thanksgiving and prayer. "The Framers understood that if we refused to recognize God's ultimate sovereignty over the state, we would be forced to recognize someone else's. It might be a king or an army. Or, as we are learning today, it might be a band of federal judges."[71] Another article put it concisely: "It is time for Congress to exercise its authority to rein in this out-of-control federal judiciary and if the courts refuse to abide by congressional limits, then Congress must impeach those runaway judges."[72]

Since activist, leftist judges have taken over the court system, it seems obvious that the founding fathers should have dealt with

---

70 Munsil, Len ".".Judge with righteous Judgment" Arizona Family Focus Nov 2003: 1

71 Jeffrey, Terence P. *The Washington Times*, 9 Mar. 2003: B3; as reported in *The Journal*, American Christian College, May 2003, 5-6.

72 Hodel, Don. "Family News from Dr. James Dobson" October 2003: 1.

many issues of minutia. But with the Christian Foundation in its glory years, with over 90 percent of the population what today we would call fundamentalist Christians, it would have seemed absurd to think that you had to codify that placing the Ten Commandments in courthouses is OK; abortion should not be allowed; Bible reading in schools and at public events was perfectly acceptable. It's like expecting them to have written a ban on cloning. That is why it is so important for Americans to go and read what these people wrote. We have to know their worldview to understand what they meant to be our civil regulation; to understand the power and the limits on power they meant to impose on the government and the freedoms they meant our people to have. (One of the best organizations to contact to find out what the founding fathers believed is: WallBuilders, P.O. Box 397 Aledo, TX 76008-0397; 817-441-6044; www.wallbuilders.org)

Once again, liberal, activist judges and the politicians who appoint and confirm them have found that if they can funnel more and more power to these judges, without any consequences to the judges for their freedom-destroying decisions (they are never "fired"), then they can completely rid our society of all facets of the things they feel are bad: Christianity, inhibitions, sexual restraint, freedom of religion, freedom of speech, a right to keep and bear arms, and all things based on a once-Christian culture. How they cannot see the unintended consequences of their actions is beyond me. Their intended consequences seem to be the eventual removal of individual freedom—all done in the name of individual freedom.

THE GAY OLIGARCHY

The judiciary is also being used to implement the homosexual agenda. Judges are making rulings that are in direct violation of law and common sense to force the homosexualization of America on us.

In Florida a woman named Linda Forsythe was forced by Judge Gerald O'Brien to give custody of her son from a previous relationship to her more recent partner, a lesbian lover, after they broke up. In relation to the partner's partial sex change operations, "Judge O'Brien ruled: 'Some jurisdictions prefer to remain in the 19th century understanding of binary sex that saw male and female as distinct, immutable, and opposite,' he wrote, adding that both marriage and gender were primarily a state of mind."[73]

In Colorado, a woman, Dr. Cheryl Clark adopted a baby girl from China. She was living with a lesbian lover at the time. When they broke up, her partner, Elsey McLeod, took her to court. "Judge John Coughlin awards her equal parenting time and near-equal decision-making authority over Dr. Clark's daughter, even though Ms. McLeod has no legal or biological relationship to the girl..... Increasingly, activist judges are forging pro-gay case law, often in the teeth of contrary statutory law."[74] Since Dr. Clark has become a Christian and no longer believes in the gay lifestyle, Judge Coughlin's ruling would prohibit her from teaching her daughter the biblical position on homosexuality because of its homophobic stance.

Many judges are making multiple pro-gay rulings that do not make news stories, setting precedents that violate laws and the will of the vast majority of the American people, but these precedents will be used to justify ever-expanding gay rights to the detriment of all other groups of Americans.

Even though only six states' legislatures have allowed gay adoption, courts in twenty states have allowed it. Whether you agree with any of the above philosophically or not, these rulings are legislating from the bench, and this is not the job of judges.

NON-LIBERAL JUDGES
NEED NOT APPLY

At the time I first started researching this book, Miguel Estrada had been nominated for a federal appeals court. The liberal Democrats filibustered the nomination. (To make it simple, I will use the term "filibuster" to include both the filibuster and the threat to filibuster.) What this does is make certain that it

---

73 Vincent, Lynn. "Judicial Preview" *World Magazine* 6 Mar 2004: 24-25.
74 Ibid.

takes 60 votes, the number to override a filibuster, to confirm a conservative judge. But without the filibuster, which has never been done by conservatives to stop a liberal judge from being appointed, it just takes 51 votes to confirm a judge. If this tactic works, it means that from now on it will take only 51 votes for liberal judges, but 60 to confirm conservative judges. Therefore, from that point on, only leftist, activist judges will be put on the federal bench, unless the Senate is overwhelmingly conservative, which is not the same as overwhelmingly Republican, since, unlike the Democratic leadership, the Republican leadership is diverse, with liberals, moderates and conservatives.

September 4, 2003 was another day that should live in infamy. I woke up, turned on the news and heard the announcement that Miguel Estrada withdrew his nomination to the appeals court. After two years of being harassed by liberal senators, after having his nomination filibustered, his name and honor besmirched; after such a long time of being constantly beat up by the liberal Democrats that do not want Hispanics in high office, he finally gave up. The liberals have won: from now on it will take 60 votes to confirm a conservative judge and only the traditional 51 to confirm a liberal activist judge. Without the American people **SCREAMING** for impeachments when an activist judge makes an anti-constitutional ruling, the Constitution is dead. *Your* freedom will end if *you* don't get involved. Only you can decide if the American people will let this treason stand. (Authors' note: The American people have started to take action! On November 2, 2004, Tom Daschle, who engineered this filibuster-to-stop-judicial-appointments-scheme was removed from office by the voters of his state! It was the first time since 1950 that the incumbent minority leader has been voted out! Hurray for all the real Americans in South Dakota!)

These judges are people who do not care about the law, will think the Constitution is irrelevant (except when useful to them), and don't care about individual rights. All they care about is their agenda and obtaining absolute power. Ironically, once they obtain the remainder of this power, I believe, without the slightest hint of gratitude, they will turn on the very politicians who guaranteed their appointments and totally subordinate these liberal politicians to their will. But gloating will not bring us much pleasure, since we will no longer be a free people and the total installation of the liberal agenda will have already made us all equally in bondage, poor and miserable. Thank God the American people are starting to do something about it. But we need so many more to actually save America. Please call your congressman to start the impeachments that are needed.

November 18, 2003: the Massachusetts Supreme Court, for all practical purposes, ruled that the state legislature has 180 days to legalize same-sex marriage. This basically declares the end of rule of law in Massachusetts and the beginning of the Oligarchy of the Judiciary in that state. Prior to this date, a court could not tell the legislature what laws to make.

The state constitutions of California and Nevada require a two-thirds majority vote in their legislatures to raise taxes. In July of 2003 the state supreme courts of both states ordered that it just take a simple majority to raise taxes. What this means is that like Florida and New Jersey and Massachusetts, these state supreme courts are declaring the end of rule of law and the beginning of rule by the courts. A court, by law, cannot order a legislature to violate its constitution! If the members of an assembly of judges so order, they must be brought up for impeachment immediately, unless rule of law is to be dispensed with. Trust me, you don't want rule of law dispensed with. A technical note: on the federal level, the House of Representatives impeaches government employees, but this does not get rid of them. It simply brings them to trial before the Senate and the Senate decides whether or not to actually remove the person from office. Therefore, if the Senate has lots of liberal senators, no liberal activist judge will ever be "fired." (Although at the state level, the process can vary, state by state.)

Most people have been brainwashed to believe that impeachment is only to be used for criminal violations by public officials. This is generally the way it has been practiced in the last few decades, but this narrow interpretation is of only recent origin. Chief Justice of the Supreme Court, Joseph Story, in 1833 described what impeachment is all about.

"There are many offences, purely *political*, which have been held to be within the reach of…impeachments, not one of which is in the slightest manner alluded to in our statute book. …the task of positive (statutory) legislation would be impracticable if it were not almost absurd to attempt it."[75] This means that many of the offenses that will bring impeachment proceedings will violate no law. The word "political" as used here does not mean exactly what it would today. Read below to learn what they meant by it.

"The offences to which the power of impeachment has been and is ordinarily applied as a remedy are…what are aptly termed *political* offences, growing out of personal misconduct, or gross neglect, or usurpation, or habitual disregard of the public interests."[76]

Most interesting for our emphasis, is the fact that over 150 years ago, it was specifically mentioned that a judge should be impeached for trying to usurp power from the other branches of government.[77] It would be wise to heed Thomas Jefferson's warning: "The germ of dissolution of our federal government is in the…federal judiciary…working like gravity by night and by day, gaining a little today and a little tomorrow, and advancing its noiseless step like a thief over the field of jurisdiction until all shall be usurped."[78]

---

75 Joseph Story; *Commentaries on the Constitution of the United States* Boston: Hilliard, Grey, and Company, 1833; Vol. II, Pg. 264, #795. As reported in: Barton, David, *Impeachment Restraining an Over Active Judiciary.* Aledo, TX, Wallbuilder's, 1996, pg. 17.

76 Story; Vol. II, Pg. 233-4, #762. As reported in: Barton, *Impeachment Restraining an Over Active Judiciary*, pg. 17.

77 Although most original references will be used for quotes, most of the factual content, not the opinion part, is from the book: Barton, Dave; *Impeachment, Restraining an Overactive Judiciary;* Aledo, TX, WallBuilders, 1996. I highly recommend purchasing this short book from Wall Builders listed in Appendix 1 in the back of this book.

78 Thomas Jefferson, *Writings of Thomas Jefferson*, Albert Ellery Bergh, editor (Washington D.C.: The Thomas Jefferson Memorial Association, 1904), Vol. XV, Pg. 331-332, to Charles Hammond on August 18, 1821. As reported in: Barton, *Impeachment Restraining an Over Active Judiciary*, pg. 15.

Article II, Section 4, Para. 1 of the Constitution states: "The President, Vice-President, and all civil officers of the United States, shall be removed from office on impeachment for, and conviction of, treason, bribery, or other high crimes and misdemeanors."

Thus, people have said that you cannot impeach unless a criminal act has been committed. But, "misdemeanors" as it was defined in the eighteenth and nineteenth centuries meant "ill behavior, evil conduct, fault, or mismanagement."[79] It was not referring to our modern-day penal codes in any sense of the term. Several of the authorities of that day referred to non-statutory misdemeanors.

Justice Story is emphatic about this point: "Congress has unhesitatingly adopted the conclusion that *no* previous statute is necessary to authorize an impeachment for any official misconduct.... In the few cases of impeachment which have hitherto been tried, *not one* of the charges has rested upon any statutable misdemeanors."[80] (emphasis added)

Even in the modern era this was understood. Representative Gerald Ford, later President Ford, put it this way: "An impeachable offense is whatever a majority of the House of Representatives considers it to be at a given moment in history; conviction results from whatever offense or offenses two-thirds of the other body considers to be sufficiently serious to require removal of the accused from office."[81]

Over the last fifty years the judiciary has blatantly violated the founder's intentions, ignored the Constitution, read into the Constitution, legislated from the bench (usurping the legislative branch's powers), vetoed legislation (usurping the executive branch's power), broken the law and reversed the outcome of direct elections by the people; most of the times that these

---

79 Webster, Noah, *An American Dictionary of the English Language* (New York: S. Converse, 1828.) As reported in: Barton, *Impeachment Restraining an Over Active Judiciary*, pg. 22.

80 Story, Vol. II, Pg. 267, #797. As reported in: Barton, *Impeachment Restraining an Over Active Judiciary*, pg. 23.

81 Impeachment and the U. S. Congress, Robert A. Diamond, editor (Washington D. C.: Congressional Quarterly Inc., 1974), Pg. 6-7. As reported in: Barton, *Impeachment Restraining an Over Active Judiciary*, pg. 25.

things were done, not one congressman brought up impeachment. According to David Barton in his book *Impeachment*, this is because the politicians see no support for this from their constituents. The media will crucify anyone in Congress who dares to mention impeaching a liberal judge. If your representatives don't know that YOU support this, they have little reason to do it. Nobody wants to fight a bunch of Goliaths alone. Remember, the House of Representatives has the power of impeachment. (The Senate tries the case afterwards.) When a judge makes these unconscionable decisions, contact your congressman and tell him you want Judge So-and-So impeached and why you want him impeached.

Once again, do not believe the *lie* that federal judges are appointed for life and there is nothing you can do about their anti-American behavior. Sixty-one federal judges or Supreme Court justices have been investigated for impeachment, of whom thirteen have been impeached.[82] You as an individual citizen have not only the right, but the duty to bring up the subject of impeachment of judges to your congressman when they violate their duties in the ways mentioned above. There is a process to go through once you have registered your complaint, but you do not have to do it, your congressman does. Frivolous impeachments are weeded out before they can do any damage. For those who worry that immoral politicians will use this to rid the country of any judge remotely right of center, remember, it takes at least two-thirds of the senators present to make an impeachment stick once the trial starts. If Americans are willing to vote in their own best interests, there won't be that many liberal senators of either party left.

Until we get back to what the founders intended, using impeachment as a check and balance against an abusive judiciary, what Justice Story warned about will continue to be true:

---

82 Barton, David. *Impeachment, Restraining an Overactive Judiciary.* Aledo, TX: WallBuilders, 1996, 10. Available directly from WallBuilders, listed in Appendix 1. I *highly recommend* you order this book.

83 Story, Vol. II, Pg. 218, #745. As reported in: Barton, *Impeachment Restraining an Over Active Judiciary*, page 15.

that impeachment will be a power "so weak and torpid as to be capable of lulling offenders into a general security and indifference."[83] These judges will only care what others think, believe, or know to be the law, if impeachment is revived.

Professor John Randolph Tucker explained, "The impeachment power was intended to cleanse the government from the presence of worthless and faithless officials."[84]

George Mason was called the "Father of the Bill of Rights." To him impeachment was warranted for "attempts to subvert the Constitution."[85] I would submit to you that as well as those things listed above, the Constitution is subverted when judges find things that are definitely not in the document. In the early '60s, judges found a right to silence prayer in schools. A year later Bible reading was outlawed in those schools by another judicial fiat. Ten years after that, they found a right to abortion in the Constitution; and thirty years after that they found a right to sodomy, as spelled out by our country's founding fathers. The six justices who ruled for this "find" should have been impeached immediately. Not just because I disagree with their agenda, as do most Americans, but because of the flagrant disregard and disrespect they obviously have for our most sacred document. People who want to make up the Constitution as they go along have no right to be making decisions on what it means. Justice Story even covered this base in his remarks: impeachment could be invoked for "attempts to subvert the fundamental laws and introduce arbitrary power."[86]

Some might fear that impeachment will interfere with the independence of the judiciary. But, "rather than violating the

---

84 John Randolph Tucker, *The Constitution of the United States; A Critical Discussion of its Genesis*, Development and Interpretation, Henry St. George Tucker, editor (Chicago, Callaghan & Co, 1899) Vol. I, Pg. 411-412 #199(f), Pg. 415, #199(o). As reported in: Barton, *Impeachment Restraining an Over Active Judiciary*, pg. 16.

85 Madison, *Papers*, Vol. III, Pg. 1528, George Mason at the Constitutional Convention on Saturday, September 8, 1787. As reported in: Barton, *Impeachment Restraining an Over Active Judiciary*, pg. 17.

86 Story, Vol. II, Pg. 268, #798. As reported in: Barton, *Impeachment Restraining an Over Active Judiciary*, pg. 17.

'independence of the judiciary,' impeachment actually gives the people a means to hinder the court from imposing its own judicially driven political agenda on them. In fact, the impeachment of a judge might properly be likened to a recall election…."[87]

Impeachment is the only way to make unelected judges accountable for their actions. You can vote against the reelection of congressmen and senators and the president, you can recall local and national politicians, but impeachment is the only way to get rid of a dictatorial judge before he feels his time is up. If we don't contact our congressmen, maybe we deserve the fate these judges have in store for us; for then we will have allowed the enslavement of our future generations.

"The Founders never intended that the judiciary would become unaccountable to the people. In fact, Thomas Jefferson warned that an unaccountable judiciary would transform our form of government into an 'oligarchy' (a nation ruled by a small council of elite individuals)."[88]

When referring to him and our other founding fathers, Dr. James Dobson said: *"They put within the constitution the responsibility in the Congress to check the courts. But Congress has totally abdicated that responsibility, and what we have now is the kind of oligarchy that Thomas Jefferson was worried about."* [89]

Until we regain control over an unfettered gang of liberal activist judges, our legislators will be completely impotent and the people of this country will be the subjects and slaves of a bunch of unelected officials who simply do not care what the will of the people is. As long as WE do not contact our congressman when judges redesign our society, throw away our heritage, and destroy our America, these arrogant despots will continue to erode your freedoms, your rights, and your opportunities to live in a country that you love.

A real catch-all case came up in *United States vs Eichman* (1990). Because people were outraged by certain desecrations of

---

87 Barton, David. *Impeachment, Restraining an Overactive Judiciary,* Aledo, TX WallBuilders, 1996, 28.
88 Ibid., 29-31.
89 Dobson, Dr. James. *Family News from Dr. James Dobson,* October 2003: 3.

the American flag, the will of the American people was made known through both national and state laws being passed making it a crime to destroy the flag in an unauthorized manner. The judges overruled the obvious will of the people and "vetoed" all such legislation. Not only is this usurping both legislative and executive power, but by going against the expressed will of the people it violates the spirit of the Constitution. We already know that many judges do not care what the Constitution says or what the founders meant. But those that are that way deserve to be impeached.

June 23, 2005: On that day the supreme court, in Kelo vs. City of New London, expanded eminent domain to allow governments to confiscate private property for the "public purpose" of creating jobs. The homes in question were not blighted. The decision allows municipalities to condemn decent homes, churches, etc., and turn land over to developers simply to enhance economic development and increase tax revenue. Justice O'Conner, in her dissenting view said, " 'The specter of condemnation hangs over all property,' she wrote. 'Nothing is to prevent the state from replacing any Motel 6 with a Ritz-Carlton, any home with a shopping mall, or any farm with a factory.' "[90] The odd feeling you are having is more of your rights being taken away.

Another way judges are usurping power is from the people directly. This is being done by judges modifying and even reversing the decisions of juries. The Seventh Amendment assures a fair and impartial trial by our peers. Yet, how often do you hear about a judge arbitrarily overturning or altering the verdict? One study recently reviewed 208 cases in one year and found that this had been done by judges in 102 of those cases.[91] If many of us contact our congressmen and still they refuse to impeach a judge, we must start recall elections to get rid of the recalcitrant politician and replace him with one that will respond to the people's will.

---

90 Chesser, Paul. "Whose Domain?" *World Magazine* 16 July 2005: 19.
91 Eric Schnapper, "Judges Against Juries—Appellate Review of Federal Civil Jury Verdicts," Wisconsin Law Review, 1989, Pg. 247. As reported in: Barton, *Impeachment Restraining an Over Active Judiciary*, pg. 46.

Unless we can convince our congressmen to once again start using the impeachment process as it was intended, we will continue to suffer the fate that Thomas Jefferson warned about when he wrote: "The Constitution…is a mere thing of wax in the hands of the judiciary which they may twist and shape into any form they please."[92]

THE NEWEST FORM OF ACTIVISM

The judiciary has just discovered a new liberal activist tactic. Lower courts are now reversing Supreme Court decisions they do not agree with.

When the Supreme Court ruled that the RICO (racketeering) statutes could not be used against pro-life demonstrators at abortion clinics, the Seventh Circuit Court later ruled that the injunction on pro-lifers that was reversed by this Supreme Court ruling must stand!

Also, District Judge Napoleon Jones ruled that the Boy Scouts must be punished for practicing the rights the Supreme Court ruled they had. These lower-court rulings, overturning Supreme Court rulings, would be another good reason for impeaching these judges.

---

92 *Jefferson Memoirs*, Vol. IV, Pg. 317, to Judge Spencer Roane in September, 1819. As reported in: Barton, *Impeachment Restraining an Over Active Judiciary*, pg. 50.

Chapter 7

Crime and Punishment

A liberal friend of mine was explaining to me why we have to have a welfare system that will enable some people to live their entire lives without working, with you and me paying all their expenses for them.

He said that he personally knew a friend who simply refused to ever work. The man would become a criminal and steal rather than work. Liberals believe that we should support such people.

A better solution would be to let them be on welfare up to two years at a time so they have the opportunity to get job training (and up to five years during their lifetime), and if they turn to crime and refuse to do anything useful with their lives, once they reach the three felony rule, we pay whatever third-world country we have made an agreement with to accept them as a new citizen. The point being, if they do not want to do their share to achieve the American dream, why should we work extra hard to hand it to them?

THE THREE FELONY RULE—Details

Since the ACLU and others have gone to such great lengths to make absolutely certain that convicted criminals are merely housed and not punished, crime has gone through the roof. We have around two million people in prisons! They just don't mind going to prison. Further, it seems impossible to reverse this trend. I have an idea that might stop recidivism without adding punishment and it will be cheaper and more effective than our present system. To pacify those who might oppose it, it even includes letting the inmates free the last half of their sentence.

First time felons would go through the same process we now employ. Capital offenses would, obviously, not be included in the Three Felony Rule. After they have paid their debt to society, they get the second chance that everybody is privileged to have in this country. However, conviction on a second felony (or second bunch of felonies if more than one charge is filed per crime) will be different.

They will go through the regular process and if convicted will be sentenced to a normal amount of time for the crime. But only one-half of that time will be served in prison. The other half they will be set free….to be a temporary citizen in a third-world country that we have a deal with.

The basics of the deal are fairly simple. We will pay a friendly third-world country between 20 percent and 50 percent of whatever it would cost to maintain the felon here for the time he has left to serve. He will be a temporary citizen of their country, not a prisoner, for that time. He will be subject to the laws of that country with the stipulation that he will be allowed freedom of religion, not being forced to participate in the politically correct religion (or non-religion) of the country. He will be required to take language lessons, if a basic necessity for that country. Although I think we will be wise enough to choose a country like Uganda, where the official language is English. He will be supplied with one meal a day that a system has been set up to provide, in case he has trouble getting a job at first. Our purpose is not to starve him, but to make him realize how valuable US citizenship is. He may not leave that country. If he violates the conditions of this situation, it is another felony.

After he has served his time, he may return to the US as a citizen. He has paid his debt to society.

If, thereafter, he is convicted of a third felony or set of felonies, he will serve his sentence in a prison in his new country, the third-world country he previously was only a temporary citizen of. Now his citizenship will be permanently there. We will pay a fraction of what it would cost to house him here with the agreement that at the end of his sentence, that government will accept him as a citizen. Upon his verified release when he completes his sentence, a final payment will be given to that country.

The purpose of this is: (1) To teach chronic criminals that the cost of membership in a free country is obeying the laws. (2) Lessen recidivism. (3) Save money. (4) Reduce overcrowding in prisons and reduce the need for so many prisons. (5) Encourage older criminals who have just come back from their temporary citizenship abroad, to tell younger people who are pursuing a life of crime, "You don't want to go where I've been."

With some of the money we save in this system, we could consider the possibility of a special anti-recidivism tactic after their return from their temporary third-world citizenship (after strike two.) The government could help them find a job in the private sector, but subsidize the housing and expenses for six months to help them get a little ahead, making up for lost time. Counseling for budget management would be free. If they wanted to get job training or education, the government could support them up to one year for that purpose. Then, like the rest of us, they are on their own. This will more than make up for the presumed blame liberals put on society for the individual's previous decision to lead a life of crime. After all, the rest of us, or our parents, had to work to support us while we got our education and training.

Chapter 8

How Any Third-World Country Can Become the Next America

(Rich, Powerful and Free)

"Virtually all the countries created after WWII, most of them in Africa, have regressed socially, politically, economically, and in virtually all other respects since freeing themselves from their colonial condition. Millions and millions have died in fratricidal wars. Millions have died of starvation and millions are condemned to die by famine and by AIDS."[93]

The Democratic Republic of Congo is an excellent example of the chaos in many countries in Africa. In September of 2002 an attack started by one of the eight militias in Congo: 500,000 were made homeless, 60,000 were killed. The eight different groups seem to be trying to gain control over the different areas of wealth in the country. In "...similar tribal conflicts in nearby Rwanda eight years ago...nearly a million died."[94]

It is important to realize that there is one large factor that stimulates the constant civil wars that have occurred since the

---

93 Joffe, Gerardo. "The UN and Israel" (Paid Advertisement) *World Magazine* 18Jan2003: 32.
94 Belz, Mindy. "Carnage in Congo" *World Magazine* 18 Jan 2003: 33.

colonial powers left Africa. When those countries conquered Africa, African colonies' borders were put in place according to how much land each European power could grab first before the others got there. As a result, when they left, the indigenous political powers that were forming just kept those borders mostly intact. This oftentimes kept tribes that had been at war with each other for hundreds of years forced to "live under the same roof" forever. Therefore, before any nation on the continent of Africa can hope to become the "next United States of America," they have to analyze if this is the root of their problem and see if by getting together with three or four of their neighbors they could redraw territorial boundaries equitably so that they wind up with about the same amount of resources, but each country includes non-warring population groups. This would be incredibly difficult—think of trying to get four guys to agree on redistributing all their possessions, let alone four nations—but it probably does have to be done to stop much of Africa from its constant march toward the next Dark Age. The four "guys" would be able to do it if they were made to understand that the only alternative would be a persistent downward spiral to total destitution and homelessness.

Once this first major hurdle has been cleared, then there really is not a reason in the world why many other countries could not attain the height that the United States of America has. This includes countries on every continent.

In America, the Christian foundation led to the honesty and integrity that made capitalism thrive, developed a Constitution whose balance of power left much less room for corruption and allowed us to evolve a freer and freer culture over time, the combination of which led to more and more wealth and power.

As I've looked at many other countries' cultures it seems like every time many of them take a few steps forward, and it looks like they will achieve wealth and power, freedom is stopped by corruption.

Historically speaking, as Biblical Christianity took hold in Europe, those countries finally came out of the dark ages and many became world powers. After WWII, the African colonies, led by those powers, started to emerge into the twentieth century. But with independence, came a rejection of many of the tenets of Western civilization, throwing out the good with the bad, and many of these countries have lost what they had gained. They are besieged by tribal hostilities, war, revolution, spread of AIDS, and economic collapse. The end of this strife is being precluded by ever increasing corruption at the national and local levels.

In recent years, Europe has rejected most of the Christian principles that still hold some sway in the USA. The main change seems to be that where many of those countries were America's equals before WWII, the US has greatly outpaced them in the last half-century or so. The bad news is that America is headed in the same direction as Europe. It is just forty or fifty years behind in this degradation.

If the liberal establishment in the USA has their way, we will be rid of all but an insignificantly small remnant of Biblical Christianity within a couple of decades—sooner if they can accomplish it more quickly. This has already been tried in other countries.

Russia, and later the United Soviet Socialist Republic, did it effectively in the early decades of the twentieth century and they became a superpower—at the cost of millions of their citizens' lives. That political entity lasted less than one-third as long as the USA has so far. Without Christianity, can honesty and integrity survive? And if they don't, capitalism is also doomed…and without wealth, we will, internationally, lose our power…and without power, freedom is much harder to retain.

Some will say, "Wait a minute, have you forgotten about a shining example that has come very far without a Christian foundation? What about the Japanese?"

Japan's religious foundation in recent centuries has been Buddhism and Shintoism, which even today comprises 84 percent of the religious belief in the country. Admittedly, honesty, integrity and a strong work ethic are also emphasized in these religions. "All occupations are Buddhist practice. Through work we are able to attain Buddhahood." "…work hard, Heaven will protect you, the gods will bestow their favor, and your profits will be exceptional."[95]

The intelligence of the Japanese is undeniable. But there is another trait which I think explains their rise to prominence. As a people, the Japanese have a national trait that is unique in the world. For over fifteen hundred years they have shown the ability to examine other cultures and other technologies, determine the best traits of those civilizations, and assimilate them into their own culture. No other people on the face of the Earth have ever been able to do this so successfully.

By assimilating capitalism, technology, etc., Japan compares quite favorably to the US. Their GDP is about one-third of the US, but so is their population. Their per capita GDP is higher than Great Britain or Germany as of 2004. They are governed by a parliamentary democracy, making them among the freest people on Earth. I believe that the overriding reason they came so far so fast is that trait to assimilate.

I congratulate the Japanese on their accomplishments, and let's face it, as a people, you've got to love them. At this point in history all I can say to put doubt in your mind about whether or not the US still needs that Christian foundation is: Ask yourself this: Will Japan's success stand the test of time? They have only been free and modern and wealthy for less than seventy years, about the time the USSR lasted. They have been in a recession since 1990, when the Japanese stock market collapsed; it has never recovered. Between 1990 and 2002 the government debt compared to GDP has more than doubled. With all my heart, I hope they do not slip back into a feudal, warlord-run system. I hope they do not lose the freedom and wealth and all of the modern luxuries we both enjoy. But if we return to our Christian foundation and they don't start forming one, I predict that forty years from now America will still be great, while they will have slipped several steps backward. On this seeming exception, only time will tell.

---

95 Shosan Suzuki as quoted in: Olasky, Marvin "Strenuous economy" *World Magazine* 14 June 2003: 85.

Third-world nations can have what America has, but it would take mass dedication to the task. By pure determination, can an entire nation will themselves to form a new government that will, as President John Quincy Adams said: "...meld the principles of Christianity with civil government"? Can they will themselves to get to know the Bible? Not meaning to over emphasize this, it is just the first step.

Then you've got to be willing to die, if need be, so that your future generations will live free. You have to renounce any corruption in your country no matter what the consequences to yourself, your family and your friends. If you do not understand why I am saying this, you need to learn more about the—to Americans unimaginable—degree of corruption in many third-world countries. The other possible half of the confusion would be a need to learn more about the incredible sacrifices of our founding fathers in taking on our own revolution.

At the same time, these citizens of an impoverished country have to take vows of personal honesty and integrity. Then they need to try to abolish greed as much as possible. (Yes, capitalism can flourish without greed—greed being the love of money. You can still like it very much.)

Then you have to adopt the rule of law. It would be wise to base it on the US Constitution. This would include impeaching judges whenever they give in to the temptation to start legislating from the bench. We did not have the guts to do that when they shyly started occasionally doing that over sixty years ago and now we get ridiculous rulings such as: "It is unconstitutional for an American to say the Pledge of Allegiance in the public schools." A ruling which is, thank God, on appeal at the time of this writing.

Additionally, you have to adopt capitalism. Letting men and women who want to work harder and/or smarter keep most of the rewards of their extra efforts. As long as what they gain is not gained through illegal or immoral means, they keep the majority of it and do with it as they will.

The final and hardest step of all for most nations would be accepting the principle that all men and all women are created equal in the eyes of God, and you would be real wise to see things His way. They will have to accept all people as equals, no matter the differences in color, race, national origin, sex, disability, cultural differences or tribal allegiance. Because of the worst human trait (other than rejection of God), the "us versus them" mentality, this is the most difficult thing for almost any human being to accept.

There is another thing that Americans take for granted that is lacking in many third-world countries: private property rights. In the US, you buy a piece of land and it is yours. It's taken for granted. In many poor nations, because of the lack of rule of law, there is no guarantee of this. A capricious decision by a local potentate or the federal government and everything you have worked for all your life can be taken away with no thought of compensation. But: Has the Kelo vs. City of New London decision to expand eminent domain taken away our private property rights in the United States? You have to decide whether or not to take a wait-and-see attitude or whether you want to contact your legislators and encourage them to pass legislation overturning this questionable ruling.

So, to make the third-world country the next America you need: (1) a strong Christian foundation, melding Christian principles with civil government; (2) capitalism, free enterprise; (3) citizens, and more especially, government officials, dedicated to honesty and integrity; (4) private property rights; (5) rule of law; (6) getting rid of as much of the "us versus them" mentality as possible. It is a hard task, but it has been done before, not perfectly or all at once, but we did do it.

Chapter 9

The Worst Human Trait

When we try to analyze human nature it is very hard to define what the worst human trait is. But in my study of history and current events, I would say that the worst human trait is the "us versus them" (UVT) mentality.

"What?" you say. "That's not that big of a deal!"

I do not think you understand the depth with which I mean this. Let's look at the first facet of this: Tolerance.

As I say elsewhere in this book, "The tolerance of pure evil is stupid." But real tolerance is one of the most necessary virtues in a free society. Because of our Christian foundation and our American culture, we are the most tolerant society ever known. It took us a while to achieve it, but we are doing real well compared to the majority of countries.

When you think of all the violent conflicts in the world throughout history, it is intolerance (part of the UVT mentality) that is at the center of most of them: country against country, race against race, tribe against tribe, religion against religion. It even took the Christian religion hundreds of years to figure out that Christ would not have condoned "religious wars." While religious wars are bad, they are sometimes necessary. The Crusades started only after several invasions by Moslems into Europe. Protestants had to fight for freedom from Catholicism in the Dutch revolt and the Thirty Years War.

If you want the United States of America to be truly free, you must do the hard work of ridding yourself of many of your intolerances. Different religions need to live side by side in peace and without animosity. To the Christians reading this book I would say that Jesus said that you must love your neighbor and do good things for them; yes, gently trying to persuade them to come to Jesus as Lord and Savior, but you cannot hate them if they choose not to come. God only sees one race, the human race. To all people, religious and non-religious alike, I would say that if you harbor any hatred toward a group of people because of their race, ethnicity, belief system or national origin, then you hate others that God considers His children as well as you.

The Bible says: "For the LOVE of money is the root of MANY evils." I hate it when so many people misquote that phrase and say instead "Money is the root of all evil." Read what it really says above again. Money is not evil and the pursuit of it is not evil. GREED (love of money) is the root of many evils, not all evils and not even the worst of evils.

In my experience the UVT trait is far more evil. Think of the hundreds of millions of men, women and children who have been murdered, raped, mutilated, denigrated, demeaned and enslaved because of it over the centuries. Unfortunately, this is not only the worst human trait; it is also one of the most common.

I do not include when preteens go through that anti-boy, anti-girl stage. I think that is just nature's way of postponing the urge to mate until it is more practical. Perhaps additionally it is a way for us to bond more properly with our same-sex role models, helping us define our masculinity or femininity.

But I do include racism, sexism, anti-religious bigotry, the hating of other groups different than one's self, whether it is expressed by cliques at work or school or condoning the slaughter of members of other tribes in Africa.

Small, snide remarks about other persons or groups of people at work may seem harmless, but it is the seed of the same trait that killed six million Jews in concentration camps in WWII (plus six million other political prisoners in those camps.) Please let us not plant that seed in ourselves or stimulate it in others.

Remember the civil conflict in Rwanda in 1994? It involved the Hutus and the Tutsis, two ancestral groups who epitomize what the UVT mentality is all about. Over 500,000 died in the actual war. Some sources say that close to 500,000 more died in the refugee camps in Zaire (Congo) and other nearby countries, of natural causes, such as cholera. In Sudan the Moslems have killed over 1.7 million in the Christian south of their country in fifteen years of civil war. In the Anatolia peninsula in the early 1900s, the Turks (Muslims) killed 1.5 million Armenians (Christians). In countries where religion was thrown out, Communist Russia, China and other countries, tens of millions were killed because they were religious or in some other way did not fit the communist "group."

This general trait to hate others, people not like us for some reason, has caused more death, more war, more inhumanity than any other thing in the human character. When you gossip about someone or feel good when someone agrees with you that someone else is bad or stupid, or ugly or fat, etc., you are participating in that worst trait on the smallest scale. You cannot help but be aware of differences, but you should never denigrate people for them.

Also, there is nothing wrong with being proud of your heritage. If you are white or black, and/or Christian or Moslem or atheist, or Irish or Japanese, or fit into any other category, it is OK to be proud of your heritage or belief system. That is not the problem. It becomes a problem when you use that pride as a tool to increase your disdain for people who do not belong to that category—your category.

The UVT mentality automatically puts you in stressful, adversarial positions with all members of groups or categories of people that you feel are different than you. UVT contributes to hate and triumphs over love. Everyone knows or has known people that they have given a measure of respect and treated nicely, yet that person will not reciprocate in kind. They still try to think the worst of you. Why? You are not a member of their clique, on the individual scale— same thing with the large scale: race, religion, ethnicity, etc. Think of the USA and the billions of dollars and millions of man hours spent helping other nations. Yet, we are one of the most hated nations on the planet. To those who chose to hate us, we are different; we are "them."

It is significant to note that we as a country have had to learn and grow to understand that the us versus them does not work.

It took almost a century to free the slaves, another sixty years to give women the right to vote, almost another half-century for civil rights. One by one we have adopted the "them" into "us." Of all the countries in the world, no other country has as much freedom to allow every color, creed, race and religion to practice their beliefs free from harassment by the powers in their country as we do. Experience and history would indicate that this only happens in a country with a Christian foundation. This is why, no matter what your belief system, you do not want to go along with those that want to destroy this foundation, those who write it out of the history books and imply to the next generation that it was never there.

But the foundation is systematically being replaced by Secular Humanism. This, in turn, is becoming increasingly intolerant of those who acknowledge our Christian heritage, or, even worse, actually have the effrontery to practice the Christian faith.

"Tolerance was an American Christian contribution to the world. Just as you drop a pebble in the pond, the ripples go out. There was tolerance first for Puritans, then Protestants, then Catholics and then Liberal Christians, then it went out completely to Jews."

"Then in the early 1900s tolerance went out to anybody of any faith, monotheists or polytheists. Finally tolerance went out to atheists, the secular humanist and anti-religious; and the last ones in the boat decided it was too crowded and decided to push the first ones out. So now we have a unique situation in America where everybody is tolerated except the ones that came up the idea."[96]

MADE UNGRATEFUL
BY US VERSUS THEM

An excellent example of how depraved and unthinking the human condition can become when we let the UVT control us is its ability to negate our feelings of gratitude.

In 1991, Kuwait was invaded by Iraq. The UN and almost every country in the world condemned this act of war. However, Desert Storm was overwhelmingly an American-won war. Around 80 percent of the equipment and personnel and funding were from the USA. The USA saved countless Kuwaiti lives and gave their country back to them. We did not take their oil as liberals had said we would. "It's a war for oil." The true American spirit reminds us "how a nation, under God, can fight to the death to defend its freedom—then pass it on to the vanquished—with love."[97]

On September 11, 2001, nineteen terrorists flew planes into American targets, including the World Trade Center (WTC). Around three thousand innocent Americans and others were killed.

When different surveys were taken, it was found out that 36 percent of the Kuwaiti citizens interviewed said that the WTC attack was justified! This just ten years after we saved many of the lives of those interviewed and saved their country for them! Further, we saved them from their fellow Muslims (part of their "us.")

(I cannot help but interject here that in the USA's drive to distance our country from God, we show exactly this degree of ingratitude for all the blessings He has bestowed on our country.)

If this world is to truly advance, instead of regress, we have to do as much as we can to divest ourselves of the UVT mentality.

---

96 Federer, Wm. J. As quoted on the TV special "American Christian Heritage" broadcast on PAX TV 4 Aug 2005.
97 Hart, Johnny. BC *Arizona Republic*: 7 Dec. 2003.

We are all one human race. People offended by such things as interracial marriages should grow up and join a more enlightened world that we can create only if we get rid of UVT. And I don't mean by getting rid of the other "groups."

We have to stop hating others who have special problems. Manic depressives, paranoid schizophrenics, homosexuals and others need treatment, not hatred. People from other countries, especially from countries that hate us, have problems, but if our reaction is just hating them back (which we rarely do), then their problem becomes our problem and that problem, because of the blinding hate, has no solution.

An example of the UVT bad effects was the O. J. Simpson trial.

It is said that the Simpson lawyer, Johnny Cochran, didn't play the race card, he played the race deck. By his harping on the hypothesis that the only reason O.J. was on trial was because he was a black man who had the unmitigated gall to be married to a white woman, Cochran stirred up racial hatred to a frenzy. Many blacks were led down an emotional trail that fixated them on O.J.'s innocence just because he was black. Many whites were whipped into a mood of racial animosity toward blacks. By Cochran's self-serving, racist manipulations, he almost single-handedly set racial relations back thirty years. The UVT was used effectively for self-aggrandizement and to win a single case. What a waste of humanity.

LET US NOT TAKE IT TO THE EXTREME

Having said that we are all brothers in God's eyes, it is important to note that people should stay within two standard deviations from the mean—don't go to extremes; as Benjamin Franklin said, "In all things moderation." For instance, I have an ultra liberal friend (UL) who has taken much of liberal philosophy to its logical conclusions. I have said, don't be racist, all people are loved by God. (He may condemn our actions and choices, but He wishes all would come to know Him, and give up our evil ways.) But, my UL friend has taken this to the extreme in the area of immigration and thrown out common sense, declaring that the United States of America should throw open its borders and let everyone who wants to come to America become (instantly) American citizens.

Can you imagine the consequences of two billion people coming here as fast as they can get here? The housing, sanitation and food distribution problems alone would be overwhelming. I think he assumes that the traditional American culture would disappear overnight and that that would be a good thing.

Think of the economic havoc of over a billion unskilled laborers, plus a glut of semi-skilled, skilled and professional workers entering the job market. What about the political consequences? If three hundred million of the new citizens voted as a block, the USA could become a Moslem theocracy, a communist country or a virtual dictatorship in very short order.

None of this mattered to my UL friend, I was just being closed-minded. (Since "you're just being closed-minded" is a sure argument-stopper for liberals, let me remind us of what C.S. Lewis said in his book, *The Abolition of Man*. "An open mind, in questions that are not ultimate, is useful. But an open mind in ultimate foundations either of theoretical or practical reason, is idiocy. If a man's mind is open on these things, let his mouth at least be shut.")

We all need a concept of "I." We need to satisfy a reasonable percentage of our ego needs to be stable. Likewise a moderate amount of "us" is OK. For instance, it is all right to be proud of being Irish, or French, Catholic or Protestant, black or white. We all have a heritage, we all need a self-concept, we all need to be unique and we are that by the combination of internalized perceptions of what we are. But when we take it to extremes, we wind up with something that is the worst human trait—the us versus them concept, and it almost always leads to destructive ends. What it destroys, is a large part of the good in humanity. Everything from personal hatred to wars to genocide is the result of UVT.

IS HATE NORMAL?

There are those who will reply to me that people need someone to hate, this is just a natural part of being human. But, why should we accept this as normal? If mankind is to maintain a higher level, shouldn't we, as individuals, strive to be better than we naturally are?

I want you to think of one of the many facets that made the movie *Groundhog Day* one of the most beautifully written screenplays I have ever "seen." It involves the part of the structure related to the growth of the main character.

In the beginning of the movie, he was a totally selfish, spoiled, self-seeking child. We watched him go through the same day many times as he grew through childhood, adolescence, and, finally, grow into other-centered maturity.

Like him, we naturally start out totally self-centered. UVT keeps us the spoiled child. Unless we get rid of it, there are parts of us that will never mature, never become a full adult. And for those who would say: "Yeah, but they (whites, blacks, Christians, Muslims, Americans, foreigners, old people, etc., pick one or two) still hate me!" I would say to you, both sides acting like spoiled children are worse than one spoiled child interacting with one mature adult. If one side starts acting maturely, eventually the other side may grow up.

I got a real shock one night at work while I was talking to a seemingly loveable old white guy at work. We were talking about how innocent most Americans are about how bad it is in many parts of the world. We presumed that most Americans are unaware that in Sudan, between 1984 and 1999, around 1.7 million, mostly non-Muslims, were murdered by the Moslem government. This led to discussions on other African countries where tribal differences have cost millions more lives, plus the AIDS epidemic and the millions dead or dying of that. I commented on how over the last few decades, since the end of colonialism, how many countries that had been about to leave third-world status and join the modern world, now had taken huge steps backward.

My older friend then shocked me by saying: "It's because the n____s are in charge." His assumption was that people of a darker skin color are vastly inferior to the white races. Suddenly, I realized a startling thing. The real reason so many countries have the civil wars—tribe versus tribe, religion versus religion, etc.—is because they have too many people there that are just like my elder acquaintance at work. The "us" is good, virtuous and smart. The "them" is bad, immoral and stupid. His attitude is the very reason why those few thirsting for power can control the masses and cause the problems in many cases. Find a "them" for the masses to hate, promise to lead the fight against "them" and become a powerful ruler. Hitler was the most famous to do it. See how well it worked! The "them" was Jews, communists and "inferior" races. If he had known where to stop the war, he might have ruled most of Europe until his natural death, sometime in the 1960s or 1970s.

Every generation will have to deal with it, but let's all try to make the worst human trait nothing more than a bad memory in human history.

Chapter 10

Right to Bear Arms

"A well regulated militia, being necessary to the security of a free State, the right of the people to keep and bear arms, shall not be infringed": US Constitution, Second Amendment.

Much of the factual data contained in this chapter is from the following report: "The Right to Keep and Bear Arms Report of the Subcommittee on the Constitution of the Committee on the Judiciary, United States Senate, Ninety-Seventh Congress, February 1982." In the footnotes, it will simply refer to this as "Report" and give page numbers.

I am constantly reminded how isolated from the rest of the world we, in the United States, are and how innocent we have become. For all history, country after country, tribe after tribe, people after people, the Earth has been populated by massive numbers of unarmed victims.

Some group has the most advanced weapons, you don't. You die, they don't.

The Harappan civilization of the Indus River Valley was one of the four "cradles of civilization." Two thousand years before Alexander the Great invaded India, some believe that civilization was the equal of Egypt, China and Mesopotamia. Yet, the illiterate, barbarian Aryans to the north had superior weaponry and they invaded and destroyed one of the four greatest cultures of that day.

Today, or in recent history, if you are talking about Sierra Leone, Congo, Sudan, Zimbabwe, Columbia, Laos, Cambodia or even China, it's a variation of the same story. When the masses are unarmed, a relatively small group of armed people can choose to either enslave the people or slaughter them.

In a review of the video documentary *Innocents Betrayed*, Dr. Paul Gallant and Dr. Joanne Eisen tell of all the evidence against gun control as it relates to genocide.[98] In the documentary, producer Aaron Zelman, et al, shows how the single greatest factor in all genocide is an unarmed citizenry. "According to criminologist Don B. Kates, 'thirty-four times more victims were killed by governments in the 20th century genocides than were murdered in all the depredations of the 20th century criminals.'"[99] "In Turkey, for example, the national gun permit system in 1911 created a list of firearms owners. When the rulers of that nation decided to exterminate the Armenian minority in 1915, it was relatively easy to find and disarm those who had gun permits. Mass murdering 1.5 million unarmed Armenians by forced death march (i.e., three-quarters of the Armenian population of Turkey) then took place with little resistance.

"The same scenario has been repeated in nation after nation. Ever-tightening gun control laws in the Soviet Union, starting in 1917, produced a population almost entirely unarmed. In the 1930s, Stalin's purges and the terror famine against the Ukrainians cost 20 million lives."[100] They go on to recount the Khmer Rouge's disarming and then killing 1.5 million of their citizens in Cambodia, nearly one-third of their population.

---

98 Gallant, Dr. Paul; Eisen, Dr. Joanne. "170,000,000 and Counting" *America's 1st Freedom.* March 2004: 30-31.

99 Ibid.

100 Ibid.

"'Never again!' is a familiar refrain. But it requires possession of the means—namely, firearms—to make such a promise stick! The mere utterance of such a phrase is otherwise meaningless."[101] The authors go on to describe how in Nazi Germany "reasonable" gun laws, licensing, registration, etc., led to confiscation and extermination. They also state that the US Gun Control Act of 1968 was based on just these German models.

China has had a tradition of forcing its population to remain unarmed, even prior to the invention of firearms, and, despite an advanced civilization and a huge population, they have been conquered by nomadic tribes, colonized by European powers, subject to dictators and cruel emperors, and finally taken over by communists. In spite of thousands of years of culture, the Chinese people have had centuries on end of not knowing what it is like to be a free people.

In Germany, Hitler convinced the legislators to pass a law to register guns. He said that this was necessary for the police to more effectively do their jobs. (Huh!) Shortly after the guns were registered, many were confiscated. As we all know, soon thereafter "undesirables" were rounded up and shipped off to concentration camps, unable to defend themselves.

Anti-Second-Amendment types use rhetoric that can be quite chilling when you think of the above paragraph. They say: "As the policing of society becomes more efficient, the need for arms for personal self-defense becomes more irrelevant."[102] Say that to the third or fourth victim of a serial rapist and see what she says.

Even founding father George Mason said: "To disarm the people" is "the best and most effective way to enslave them."

Benjamin Franklin put it more cleverly when he said: "Democracy is two wolves and a lamb voting on what to have for lunch. Liberty is a well-armed lamb contesting the vote."

Please understand this: There is no foolproof system. One cannot be created. Quit falling for the implied "we can make a

---

101 Ibid.
102 Report, Pages 128-129.

perfect system" argument. Someone falls through the cracks no matter what you try. So don't throw away a system ("the right to bear arms shall not be infringed") that worked for almost two hundred years and has been shown to be better than any other. Many times a year someone will abuse their right to keep and bear arms. But it is still better than leaving everyone helpless to those who break the law; and on rare occasions this includes those appointed to enforce the law. (Refer to KKK law in this chapter.) In the last century, worldwide, dozens of times as many people died due to lack of being armed than died because of having a right to bear arms.

"Consider the Jan. 16, 2002, law school shooting in Grundy, Va. There, a student went on a shooting spree, killing the school dean, a professor and a student and wounding three others.

"Tracy Bridges, a student at the school, heard gunfire while in a classroom and ran to his vehicle to retrieve a pistol. He approached the shooter and forced him to drop his firearm before anyone else could be injured or killed.

"Had Bridges not had the firearm in his vehicle, the shooter could have continued his rampage indefinitely, or at least until the police arrived. By having a firearm on the premises—in a locked vehicle in the parking lot—an individual stopped a killing spree that could have claimed many more lives.

"...A firearm on the premises doesn't increase the risk of violence; it acts as a major deterrent and, in the most extreme cases, as the one thing that may save many lives."[103]

AN INDIVIDUAL RIGHT

Let's see how open the founding fathers were to gun control. What did the men who wrote the founding documents and signed them mean by "...the right of the people to keep and bear arms shall not be infringed."?

"To preserve liberty, it is essential that the whole body of the people always possess arms, and be taught alike, especially when

---

103 Smith, Blaine. "Thank God Tracy Bridges Wasn't a Whirlpool Employee"
    America's 1st Freedom Jan. 2005: 26.

young, how to use them." (Richard Henry Lee, Virginia delegate to the Continental Congress, initiator of the Declaration of Independence, and member of the first Senate, which passed the Bill of Rights.)

As was previously quoted: "Democracy is two wolves and a lamb voting on what to have for lunch. Liberty is a well-armed lamb contesting the vote."(Benjamin Franklin, who helped draft the Declaration of Independence, the Constitution, signed the Treaty of Alliance with France and the Treaty of Paris, ending the Revolutionary War.)[102]

"The great object is that every man be armed...Everyone who is able may have a gun." (Patrick Henry said this in the Virginia Convention on the ratification of the Constitution.)

"[The] Constitution shall never be construed...to prevent the people of the United States who are peaceable citizens from keeping their own arms." (Samuel Adams)

"No free man shall ever be debarred the use of arms." (Thomas Jefferson)

And we all remember how George Mason said that when the British plotted "to disarm the people" it was "the best and most effective way to enslave them."

The above quotes from the founding fathers of our country make it ridiculously clear that the right to bear arms refers to individual citizen's right and has nothing to do with the National Guard or some other similar organization. As if to reinforce this concept, "In the Militia Act of 1792, the second Congress defined 'militia of the United States' to include almost every free adult male in the United States."[103] These persons were obligated by law to possess a firearm and a minimum supply of ammunition.

Senator Hatch, in his preface to this report makes one of the wisest statements I have ever heard as an American. He says, "I...repudiate the approach of those who believe to solve American problems you simply become something other than

104 As reported in: Galles, Gary M. "Franklin's Yardstick of LIberty" *America's 1st Freedom* April 2003: 72.
105 Report, page vii.

American." To this he adds: "To my mind, the uniqueness of our free institutions, the fact that an American citizen can boast freedoms unknown in any other land, is all the more reason to resist any erosion of our individual rights."[106]

The Senate subcommittee goes on to report: "The Senate in the process indicated its intent that the right be an individual one, for private purposes, by rejecting an amendment which would have limited the keeping and bearing of arms to bearing 'for the common defense.'"[107]

William Rawle's "View of the Constitution" was first published in 1825 and stated, "No clause in the Constitution could by a rule of construction be conceived to give to Congress a power to disarm the people."[108] Keep in mind that Rawle was a friend of and corresponded with Thomas Jefferson. Many writers of the time, including some who worked in the founding political bodies of our country, wrote that the right to keep and bear arms was essential to warding off tyranny. It is ironic that because of the wisdom the founding fathers put in our basic documents, Americans are extremely naive about any government's tendency to become all powerful, usurping all the rights of its people. Most Americans would probably feel like saying, "That's ancient history, not the modern world." But if you even just look at the last thirty years, there are dozens of countries where this has happened or continues to happen.

"The framers of the Bill of Rights consistently used the words 'right of the people' to reflect individual rights—as when these words were used to recognize the 'right of the people' to peaceably assemble, and the 'right of the people' against unreasonable searches and seizures..."[109]

"The conclusion is thus inescapable that the history, concept, and wording of the second amendment to the Constitution of the United States, as well as its interpretation by every major commentator and court in the first half-century after its ratification,

---

106 Report, page viii.
107 Report, page 6.
108 Report, page 7.
109 Report, page 11.

indicates that what is protected is an individual right of a private citizen to own and carry firearms in a peaceful manner."[110]

To note how state constitutions defer to the Federal Constitution, it would be good to look at: re Brickey, 8 Ida. 597, at 598-99, 70 p. 609 (1902): "The second amendment to the federal constitution is in the following language: 'A well-regulated militia, being necessary to the security of a free state, the right of the people to keep and bear arms, shall not be infringed.' The language of section 11, article I of the constitution of Idaho is as follows: 'The people have the right to bear arms for their security and defense, but the legislature shall regulate the exercise of this right by law.' Under these constitutional provisions, the legislature has no power to prohibit a citizen from bearing arms in any portion of the state of Idaho, whether within or without the corporate limits of cities, towns, and villages."[111] As you can see, thanks to the Fourteenth Amendment, the part of the Idaho constitution that violated the Second Amendment was made null by the Federal Constitution.

In *Wilson v. State*[112] it says: "If cowardly and dishonorable men sometimes shoot unarmed men with army pistols or guns, the evil must be prevented by the penitentiary and gallows, and not by a general deprivation of constitutional privilege."[113] I understand the man wanting to vary the language, but realize that the word "privilege" should be replaced with the word "right."

Further supporting our freedoms, in *Simpson v. State*[114] "…By this clause of the constitution, an express power is given and secured to all the free citizens of the State to keep and bear arms for their defense, without any qualification whatever as to their kind or nature…."[115]

Bliss v. Commonwealth[116] (on the right to bear arms)…"if any portion of that right be impaired, immaterial how small the

---

110 Report, page 12.
111 Report, page 16.
112 33 Ark. 557, a 560, 34 Am. Rep. 52 at 54 (1878).
113 Report, pages 16 & 17.
114 13 Tenn. 356, at 359-60 (1833).
115 Report, page 17.
116 12 Ky. (2 Litt.) 90, at 92 & 93, 13 Am. Dec 251 (1822).

part may be, and immaterial the order of time at which it be done, it is equally forbidden by the constitution." [117]

Rep. Benjamin F. Butler (R, Mass.) made a report shortly after the Civil War that due to the violence perpetrated against blacks, the "Anti-KKK act" must include the right of blacks (and whites) to keep and bear arms as "necessary for protection against the militia but also against local law enforcement agencies."[118]

"Noting instances of 'armed confederates' terrorizing the negro, the report stated that 'in many counties they have preceded their outrages upon him by disarming him, in violation of his right as a citizen to "keep and bear arms," which the Constitution expressly says shall never be infringed.'"[119] The provision in the bill became: "That whoever shall, without due process of law, by violence, intimidation, or threats, take away or deprive any citizen of the United States of any arms or weapons he may have in his house or possession for the defense of his person, family, or property, shall be deemed guilty of a larceny thereof, and be punished as provided in this act for a felony."[120]

In other words, in this country, certain governmental powers disarmed law-abiding citizens, and the result was an increase in the power of criminals over honest people. The criminals, in this case, included members of the sheriff's department! This type of thing happens in many countries throughout time. When will we ever learn?

To reinforce this concept, on page 104 and 105 of the report, Rep. William L. Stoughton (R., Mich.) was quoted as having said: "If political opponents can be marked for slaughter by secret bands of cowardly assassins who ride forth with impunity to execute the decrees upon the unarmed and defenseless, it will be fatal to…civil liberty."[121]

---

117 Report, page 17.

118 Report, page 72.

119 1464 H. R. Rep. No 37, 41st Cong., 3rd session, 3 (Feb 20, 1871); Report, 72-73.

120 Cong. Globe, 42nd Cong., 1st session, 174 (Mar 20, 1871); Report, 73. The exact wording of this section was deleted when it was found to be redundant, Report, 104.

121 Ibid. at 321 (Mar. 28, 1871).

The report goes on to state, for those who wish to exaggerate the Second Amendment in order to defeat it, that the right to bear arms is "not a right to commit assault or otherwise engage in criminal conduct with arms by pointing them at people or wantonly brandishing them about so as to endanger others."[122]

In Federalist No. 46, James Madison, whose task it was to write the Bill of Rights, discussed how a standing army, which he distrusted, might be controlled: "To these [troops] would be opposed a militia...of citizens.... Besides the advantage of being armed which the Americans possess over the people of almost every other nation.... the governments [of Europe] are afraid to trust the people with arms."[123]

Alexander Hamilton, in Federalist No. 29 said that a standing "army can never be formidable to the liberties of the people, while there is a large body of citizens...who stand ready to defend their rights."

"Hamilton evidently felt that the militia composed of the body of the people would provide a deterrent to a federal standing army or the organized militia, only because the people had the right to keep and bear arms."[124]

During the debate over the first drafts of the Second Amendment, it was changed from its original form. This phrase was dropped: "but no person religiously scrupulous of bearing arms shall be compelled to render military service in person."[125] This was because Congressman Elbridge Gerry of Massachusetts objected on the grounds that the government could arbitrarily declare a man religiously scrupulous and also deny him the right to bear arms. He said, "I am apprehensive, sir, that this clause would give an opportunity to the people in power to destroy the Constitution itself. They can declare who are those religiously scrupulous, and prevent them from bearing arms."[126] To one of the men who helped craft the Second

---

122 Report, page 74.
123 Report, page 86.
124 Report, page 86-87.
125 Report, page 87.
126 Report, page 87.

Amendment in its final form, to take away the individual right
to keep and bear arms was "to destroy the Constitution itself."
And I believe that today's "gun safety" (formerly known as "gun
control") lobby knows this full well, agreeing with it completely.
In the 1930s we had a liberal establishment. The first federal gun
control laws were passed. In the 1960s the present liberal establishment took control from the intervening conservative establishment and many more, both national and local, gun control
laws have been passed. The remnants of the Constitution have
left some power in the hands of the people, and that cannot be
tolerated by these people most recent to acquire power.

Gerry went on to explain: "Whenever Governments mean
to invade the right and liberties of the people, they always
attempt to destroy the militia...."[127]

"Gerry plainly understood in making his proposal that one
purpose of the amendment was to ensure the existence of the
militia composed of the body of the people, since the organized
militia was subject to federal service. Therefore it was necessary
to protect the right of all people, that is, each individual, to keep
and bear arms."[128]

"The Senate...soundly rejected a proposal to insert the
phrase 'for the common defense' after the words 'bear
arms'...thereby emphasizing that the purpose of the Second
Amendment was not merely to provide for the common
defense, but also to protect the individual's right to keep and
bear arms for his own defense and self-preservation."[1279]

In *State v. Kessler,*[130] the Supreme Court of Oregon stated:
"We are not unmindful that there is current controversy over
the wisdom of a right to bear arms, and that the original moti-
vations for such provision might not seem compelling if
debated as a new issue. Our task, however, in construing a constitutional provision, is to respect the principles given the status of constitutional guarantees and limitations by the drafters;

---

127 Report, page 88.
128 Report, page 88.
129 Report, page 88.
130 289 Or. 359, 614 P2d 94, 95 (1980); Report, 90.

it is not to abandon these principles when this fits the needs of the moment." This simply means that when we try to interpret the Constitution, we have to do the research to find out what they meant when they wrote it, not what we want them to have meant.

Keep in mind that the Fourteenth Amendment insures that the limitations on the federal government's power over the people (in the Constitution) extend those limitations to the states. Therefore, the states cannot prevent the people from keeping and bearing arms. Not legally, at least.

"In 1814, Jefferson further observed that 'we cannot be defended but by making every citizen a soldier, as the Greeks and Romans who had no standing armies.'"[131]

The closer a writer is to the era of the writing of the founding documents, to a certain degree, the closer the writers' understanding of those documents. William Rawle wrote in his *A View of the Constitution,* "The corollary, from the first position, is, that the right of the people to keep and bear arms shall not be infringed.

"The prohibition is general. No clause in the Constitution could by any rule of construction be conceived to give to congress a power to disarm the people. Such a flagitious attempt could only be made under some general pretense by a state legislature. But if in any blind pursuit of inordinate power, either should attempt it, this amendment may be appealed to as a restrain on both."[132] The Fourteenth Amendment made even this attempt by a state to disarm its citizens unquestionably unconstitutional.

The subcommittee report continues that Rawle's analysis shows that in the second clause of the Second Amendment, "...the individual right to keep and bear arms encourages a militia system, and independently as recognition of a fundamental right to have arms unrestrained by state no less than federal legislation."[133]

---

131 *The Jefferson Cyclopedia,* 551 (1900); Report, 96.
132 Rawle, W. *A View of the Constitution,* 125-6, (1829); report 96
133 Report, 96.

A case in Kentucky, decided in 1822 shows the mood of a generation still familiar with the founding fathers. In *Bliss v. Commonwealth*,[134] discussing wearing weapons, the court reasoned: "The right existed at the adoption of the constitution; it had then no limits short of the moral power of the citizens to exercise it, and in fact consisted in nothing else but in the liberty of the citizens to bear arms. Diminish that liberty, therefore, and you necessarily restrain the right; and such is the diminution and restrain, which the act in question most indisputably imports, by prohibiting the citizens wearing weapons in a manner which was lawful to wear when the constitution was adopted."[135]

In a Tennessee case, referring to the state constitution and the clause which refers to the right to bear arms continues: "By this clause of the constitution, an express power is given and secured to all the free citizens of the State to keep and bear arms for their defense, without any qualification whatever as to their kind or nature...."[136]

On Page 99 of the subcommittee report it states: "In the Texas case of Cockrum v. State,...[137] the Court explained that the object of the Second Amendment was that 'the people cannot be effectually oppressed and enslaved, who are not first disarmed.'[138] The report added:

"The right of a citizen to bear arms, in lawful defense of himself or the State, is absolute. He does not derive it from the State government. It is one of the 'high powers' delegated directly to the citizen, and 'is excepted out of the general powers of government.' A law cannot be passed to infringe upon or impair it, because it is above the law, and independent of the lawmaking power."[139]

Too many Americans have accepted the false notion that we get our rights from government. What they forget is that "we the

---

134 2 Litt. (KY) 90, 13 Am. Dec 251 (1822).
135 Report, 97.
136 Report, 98.
137 24 Tex. 394 (1859).
138 Ibid @401.
139 Ibid @401-2.

people" created the government, and gave the government its power to do certain things for us. The government only has what we gave it. Our freedoms are God-given—they're our birthright. The Bill of Rights and the Second Amendment merely protect what was already given us by God. Many of those who wish to deprive the rest of us of our rights also fight against public acknowledgment of God because they understand this principle.

"...Sadly, when people think of their rights as conferred on them by government, it ultimately forces them to regard themselves as victims. It engenders an attitude of 'there's nothing I can do.' When anti-gun groups lie to women to make them so afraid of owning and learning to use firearms that women choose to remain defenseless against criminal attack—I think that's wrong, it's evil. Those who spread such lies should be exposed for what they are.

"...Our forefathers fought and died to give us the right to be involved in the political process. They knew that if you aren't involved, someone else will make the decisions and you will have to live with them."[140]

The "brilliant" Ninth Circuit Court, so famous for ruling the reciting, in public schools, of the Pledge of Allegiance unconstitutional, has now ruled, in *Siveira v. Lockyer* that the Second Amendment does not protect the individual right to keep and bear arms. Will somebody please impeach these clowns?

"It's important to note that all rights under the Constitution are vested in individuals. The authors refer to 'rights' of states only as 'powers.' In fact, the 'people' mentioned in the Second Amendment right to keep and bear arms are the very same 'people' mentioned in the First Amendment right to freedom of speech and the Fourth Amendment right of protection from unreasonable search and seizure."[141] Obviously, these all refer to individuals.

Judge Reinhardt quotes the founding fathers to support his majority opinion. This makes him sound scholarly, but those

---

140 Froman, Sandra, One on One with Sandra Froman, *America's 1st Freedom*: Feb 2003: 15.
141 Chesnut, Mark "Justice in Flames" *America's 1st Freedom* Feb 2003: 35-37, 50.

same founders said these things as well: Patrick Henry: "The great object is, that every man be armed...Everyone who is able may have a gun." George Mason: "I ask, Who are the militia? They consist now of the whole people, except a few public officers....To disarm the people is the best and most effectual way to enslave them." And add what John Adams believed to these: "Arms in the hands of individual citizens may be used at individual discretion...in private self-defense."

Forgive me for being so redundant, but if you see what the anti-gun lobby says month after month, in this court decision (of leftist, activist judges), that periodical article, those interviews; we Second Amendment believers are forced to repeat: "Just read what the founding fathers said!"

All that has been said so far should prove beyond any shadow of a doubt that the original intent was that the Second Amendment guarantees an individual right to keep and bear arms. Yet, in the part of the subcommittee report that tells of the gun-control advocates' position, one of them states: "...there is nothing to stop an outright congressional ban on private ownership of all handguns and all rifles."[142] It does not matter what the founding fathers said, it does not matter what the Constitution says, the evidence is irrelevant to these people, the gun-control types will have the rest of us obey their will no matter what!

DETERRENT

Unfortunately, other than the National Rifle Association (NRA), no national sources that I know of report stories of honest citizens preventing crimes with their privately owned guns. Therefore, most people are unaware that this happens literally thousands of times each month; most of the time the crime is stopped just by the appearance of the weapon in the intended victim's hand. No one is actually hurt! I will expand on this later.

Also keep in mind that when the infamous Snipers of 2002 decided to go on their killing spree they were in the Northwest

---

142 *Hasting Constitutional Law Quarterly*, Vol. 2, No 1, Winter 1975; Report, 170.

where gun control has made less "progress." They drove all the way to the East Coast where most of those states have for all practical purposes, disarmed their law-abiding citizens. The snipers may have been trying to minimize their chances of being shot back at.

GUN CONTROL IS UNCONSTITUTIONAL

The vast, overwhelming majority of gun control (now called "Gun Safety") laws in the US today are unconstitutional. Some common sense laws are OK, but they would be able to be counted on your fingers. The NRA estimates that if you count all federal, state and local gun control laws they number around 20,000! Few people have that many fingers.

Minors' right to bear arms can be restricted by their parents until they reach majority and move out of the house. If someone is convicted of a misdemeanor that is related to weapons or violence, access to weapons could be restricted. Of course, if you are convicted of almost any felony, you could be barred from owning or being in possession of a firearm for a reasonable time, in severe cases up to life. Additionally, a person suffering from relevant physical or mental conditions could be restricted in access to firearms. Even the Constitution does not rule out common sense. Although the term "common sense" is radically redefined by gun control advocates to mean something entirely different than it has always meant before. It means "sound prudent judgment." They define it to mean "installing the liberal agenda."

By knowing the intent of the framers of the Constitution and their repeated appeals to avoid tyranny by keeping the people armed, it becomes obvious that gun registration and licensing is unconstitutional. If these processes become law, how easy will it then be for several officials to show up at your door and demand your weapons (confiscation)? You laugh; you say, "It can't happen here." But it has happened in several countries, just in the last ten years. Ever hear of a country called Australia? Ever hear of that "stone age" country called England? These places, and others, have proven that registration leads to confiscation. Taking England as the example:

"In the beginning, when licensed gun owners fought valiantly to stave off confiscation of their registered handguns, the government threw them a bone—it *only* banned guns of a bore size larger than .22.

"When honest British licensed gun owners turned in their 'large bore' handguns—38s, .25 ACPs, 9 mms, .45s, .50s and everything in between, all slated for destruction—they hoped it would be the end of it. Indeed, they were told they could keep their .22s, but only in government-approved lockups at government-certified gun clubs.

"Yet, that 'bore reduction' gun control had barely been in place when the poor Brit handgun owners were told the government was going to collect their registered private property from the approved armory sites. The rest, as they say, is history."[143]

Looking once again to what the courts of those early days of the USA were doing we find: "...The Supreme Court of Alabama stated that 'A statute which, under the pretense of regulation, amounts to a destruction of that right (to keep and bear arms), or which requires arms to be so borne as to render them wholly useless for the purpose of defense, would be clearly unconstitutional.'"[144] In *Nunn v. State*, the US Supreme Court ruled that an 1837 law passed in Georgia which outlawed certain types of pistols was unconstitutional under the Second Amendment.

In *People v. Zerillo*[145]: "The provision in the Constitution granting the right to all persons to bear arms is a limitation upon the power of the Legislature to enact any law to the contrary. The exercise of a right guaranteed by the Constitution cannot be made subject to the will of the sheriff."

In *State v. Kerner*[146]: "We are of the opinion, however, that 'pistol' ex vi termini is properly included within the word 'arms' and that the right to bear such arms cannot be infringed. The

---

143 Norell, James O. E. "Big-Bore Smokescreen," *America's 1st Freedom*, April 2005: 41.

144 *State v Reid*, 1 Ala 612, 35 Am. Dec. 44 (1840).

145 219 Mich. 635, 189 N.W. 927 at 928 (1922): Report, 16.

146 181 N.C. 574, 107 S. E. 222, at 224 (1921): Report, 16.

historical use of pistols as 'arms' of offense and defense is beyond controversy."

"The maintenance of the right to bear arms is a most essential one of every free people and should not be whittled down by technical constructions."[147]

Both *US v. Cruikshank*[148] and *Presser v. Illinois*[149] are often cited as precedent for limiting the right to bear arms. But both cases conclude that the Second Amendment only limits the federal government; the states can do what they want. The Fourteenth Amendment effectively nullifies these decisions. Presser additionally states: "The court did not approve of an armed population as a balance to governmental power." So what? The founding fathers said they did! Even as early as the last half of the nineteenth century, megalomaniac judges were trying to change the Constitution with a wave of their magic wand.

In writing this chapter, it became more and more obvious that even court opinions after 1840 are irrelevant regarding the Second Amendment. You have to go by what the writers of the Constitution and its amendments and those who ratified it meant. Then, if you do not agree with it, you have to pass another amendment to nullify the second one. I would highly recommend against this.

MILITIA

Title 10, Section 311 of the United States Code: "The militia of the United States consists of all able-bodied males at least 17 years of age and…under 45 years of age who are, or who have made a declaration of intention to become citizens of the United States.

"(b) The classes of the militia are: (1) The organized militia, which consists of the National Guard and the Naval Militia; and (2) The unorganized militia which consists of the members of the militia who are not members of the National Guard or the Naval Militia." Now you can quibble all day long, doing mental

---

147 Ibid.
148 92 U.S. 542 (1876); Report: 10.
149 116 U. S. 252 (1886); Report: 10.

and literary gymnastics trying to find some meaning to unorganized militia that will fulfill the "gun safety" groups wishful thinking that it does not mean ordinary citizens, but that is the simplest and most obvious meaning. And if that which is obvious is also true, then the citizen has the individual right to keep and carry his gun, whether or not he belongs to the National Guard.

Those who keep on saying that the Second Amendment, since it mentions the word "militia," only refers to members of the National Guard are either ignorant or choose to ignore that the National Guard was founded over one hundred years after the ratification of the Second Amendment. How on Earth could they have been referring to something that would not exist for over a century in their future?

Why is it necessary to remind anyone that we are talking about a document written before 1800? What was the militia then? It was Paul Revere riding from town to town yelling something like, "To arms, to arms, the British are coming, the British are coming." If no one had privately owned guns, we would still be second-class British subjects.

"...the 'militia' itself referred to a concept of a universally armed people, not to any specifically organized unit. When the framers referred to the equivalent of our National Guard, they uniformly used the term 'select militia' and distinguished this from 'militia.'

"The Second Amendment right to keep and bear arms, therefore, is a right of the individual citizen to privately possess and carry in a peaceful manner firearms and similar arms."[150]

"The conclusion is thus inescapable that the history, concept, and wording of the second amendment to the Constitution of the United States, as well as its interpretation by every major commentator and court in the first half-century after its ratification, indicates that what is protected is an individual right of a private citizen to own and carry firearms in a peaceful manner."[151]

---

150 Report: 11.
151 Report: 12.

CARRYING CONCEALED WEAPONS[152]

If it is determined that CCWs are necessary (see footnote below), then there should be a CCW system in every state in the union and a reciprocal agreement that if you have one in one state, it is good in the other states as well. CCW laws work fine in the thirty-eight states that presently have them because they require significant, but not arduous, training and testing to qualify for them, not to mention a background check. The average citizen, with a little effort and study can qualify for one. A small fee to cover costs is appropriate, but there should be no annual fee for renewal of a CCW, that being an infringement on the right to bear arms. The only reason I am compromising by saying that requiring some training for a CCW is OK is that we have lost much of our father-to-child-gun-training tradition. Many parents would not know how to teach their kids about guns; and there are people out there who do not have the common sense to get training before carrying a deadly weapon.

Will a few nuts get CCWs? Probably, but remember that history shows that for every few hundred or few thousand that die because ordinary citizens are armed, a few million can die if the citizens are disarmed.

Keep in mind that in *Bliss v. Commonwealth*[153] in 1822, an appeals court in Kentucky struck down a carrying concealed weapon statute as too restrictive and, therefore, a violation of the Second Amendment. Thus, even the NRA's proud example of a return to Second Amendment freedoms, the CCW permits, were considered unconstitutional—-you should not need a permit to legally carry a concealed weapon if you have no criminal record or illegal intentions.

INTERNATIONAL GUN CONTROL "SUCCESSES"

Success for this section is being defined as the successful implementation of gun control.

---

152 A permit for carrying a concealed weapon is colloquially called a CCW.
153 12 Ky. (2 Litt.) 90, at 92, and 93. 13 Am. Dec. 251 (1822); Report: 17.

Disarming of the honest citizens was done in several countries in the twentieth century, the most famous being Germany, the USSR, and China. In each case the homicide rate in the US was tens of thousands, the homicide rate in those countries was millions. This does not strike me as something we should emulate. Might we be better off NOT repeating the mistakes of the past?

People say, "But what about school shootings and other nuts that go off the deep end with guns? What about murders and suicides that could be reduced if guns were illegal? Besides, this is America, and we don't have to worry about a totalitarian regime taking over."

We already know what happens when guns are banned. Britain has made gun ownership virtually illegal. "Three years after England banned all handguns, the use of handguns in crime jumped by 40 percent."[154] Now your chance of being the victim of a felony in London, in any one year is 26 percent! Only the criminals have guns. As a matter of fact, intended victims of criminals are now being incarcerated instead. To show how ridiculous gun control eventually gets, look at what could well be in store for us if we continue to ignore our Second Amendment rights. The following story is from gun-free England:

"Witness the story of Tony Martin, a 54-year-old farmer, whose home on the 350-acre rural tract had been...broken into...at least two dozen times. On...Aug. 21, 1999, Martin heard burglars inside his home and confronted the criminals with a shotgun. He wounded one thief and killed another. A third house breaker got away." The least of the three "had been arrested for 29 different crimes including burglary, theft and assaulting police." The other two had worse records. Martin (the victim of the burglary) was convicted of murder and sentenced to life in prison. On appeal this was reduced to manslaughter and seven years in prison. Not only was the wounded burglar interviewed as to whether or not he felt Martin should be allowed the opportunity for parole, the British government gave

---

154 LaPierre, Wayne R. "Fugitive from Injustice" *America's 1st Freedom* Oct 2003: 54.

the burglar 5000 pounds "of taxpayers' money...to fund a law suit against Tony Martin."[155]

As hard as it is to see from most American's perspective, the above story does represent the logical consequences of being a gun control society.

Australia, as well as England, has some of the strictest gun safety (gun control) laws in the world. Since they have disarmed their law-abiding citizens, crimes by armed criminals have skyrocketed.

Just for a moment, let's get a bit Orwellian. Oh, sorry, they're already Orwellian; we have to go beyond that to extrapolate.

Suppose some only half-sane dictator decides that old imperialist England is a prize worth having. He realizes that they have disarmed their people, so only police and a small army have weapons. He might then (especially if it is an oil-rich country) order some large ships, perhaps oil tankers that have not been used yet, load them with his army, pretend they are just delivering oil to petroleum-starved Great Britain, and as soon as they dock at various ports, tens of thousands of troops disembark, slaughtering millions of defenseless people and taking over the country.

Now suppose a fully insane dictator tries the same plan with the USA. Even if they had some plan that could defeat our military and police, I believe that no army on Earth could then defeat over 65 million armed Americans.

The point being: Do we have to wait until most other countries have disarmed their citizens and then watch as either their own government or some foreign power slaughters countless unarmed innocent people before we see the folly of the gun control movement? It is because it hasn't happened in Europe recently that we take no note of such things. It has already happened innumerable times around the globe in Asia, Africa and South America. And it did happen in Germany in the 1930s. If you look at current events in Sierra Leone, Congo,

---

155 LaPierre, Wayne R. "The Big Hole in British Gun Control" *America's First Freedom*. Oct 2002: 34-38.

Zimbabwe, Sudan, et al, it is happening right now! Why would we want to follow their examples and disarm our law abiding citizens? (I do include in this category all countries with disarmed citizens, whether disarmed by government fiat or poverty or other reasons.)

INFRINGEMENTS

In the section of the subcommittees report entitled "Enforcement of Federal Firearms Laws from the Perspective of the Second Amendment," I discovered startling infringements on individual rights.[156]

Under the liberal FDR administration, anti-gun legislation started being introduced at the federal level for the first time. Before 1934 there was no significant involvement of the federal government in gun regulation. The National Firearms' Act of 1934 and the Federal Firearms' Act of 1938 required a $200 excise tax on the sale of fully automatic weapons and 'sawed-off' shotguns and rifles. The identification of the buyer and seller had to be recorded. People in the business of selling firearms had to be licensed and pay a $1 fee for the license. Names and addresses of customers had to be kept.

The Gun Control Act of 1968 put more restrictions on the sale of not only handguns, but rifles and shotguns as well.

The increased need for enforcement led to the massive expansion of an obscure division under the Department of the Treasury which grew up into its own Bureau—the Bureau of Alcohol, Tobacco and Firearms (BATF).

The division's main job had been putting moonshiners out of business. But a rise in sugar prices put most of them out of business by the 1970s; the number of raids had dropped from 15,000 in 1956 to 609 in 1976. Thus, the much larger BATF switched to concentrating on firearms law enforcement.

"Although Congress adopted the Gun Control Act with the primary object of limiting access of felons and high-risk groups to firearms, the overbreadth of the law has led to neglect of precisely this area of enforcement.

---

156 Report, 19-23.

"The Subcommittee received evidence that BATF has primarily devoted its firearm's enforcement efforts to the apprehension, upon technical; malum prohibitum charges of **individuals who lack all criminal intent and knowledge.**"[157] (Emphasis added.)

The agency has ruined the lives of law-abiding citizens with felony convictions on technical violations of obscure rules, confiscated gun collections of innocent people who then had to spend thousands of dollars in court to clear their names and even then the guns often were never returned to them, even after acquittal. In spite of the Senate's repeated warning to the agency (BATF), it continued in that direction, and years after this report was written, gave us Ruby Ridge and the Waco, Texas fiasco (Branch Davidians).

The report continues by stating that "agents have tended to concentrate upon collector's items rather than 'criminal street guns.'

"…it is apparent that enforcement tactics made possible by current firearms' laws are constitutionally, legally, and practically reprehensible."[158]

In conclusion, on pages 22 and 23 the report summarizes by saying: "…the Bureau has disregarded rights guaranteed by the constitution and laws of the United States.

"It has trampled upon the Second Amendment by chilling exercise of the right to keep and bear arms by law-abiding citizens.

"It has offended the fourth amendment by unreasonably searching and seizing private property.

"It has ignored the Fifth Amendment by taking private property without just compensation and by entrapping honest citizens without regard for their right to due process of law….

"…75% of BATF gun prosecutions were aimed at ordinary citizens who had neither criminal intent nor knowledge, but were enticed by agents into unknowing technical violations. (In one case, in fact, the individual was being prosecuted for an act which the Bureau's acting director had stated was perfectly lawful.)"[159]

---

157 Report, 21. Emphasis is mine.
158 Report, 20.
159 Report: 22 & 23.

NATIONAL RIFLE ASSOCIATION

When you want to know about one particular facet of the political debates, it is best to go to a single-issue advocacy group. Obviously for Second Amendment information, the NRA is the best. But as you become more politically active, you have to develop caution and not just be a follower of everything that these groups say.

I was shocked one day when I received a political endorsement sheet from the NRA. It was trying to give its support to pro-Second Amendment candidates at the local level. It was asking NRA members to vote for good right-to-bear-arms candidates. The first two people were pro-traditional American values types. However, the third endorsement was for a candidate whose only claim to fame locally was that he was known to be the biggest liar in local politics and during his first term in office he introduced pro-homosexual bills and a bill to cancel school choice. Then in his campaign for reelection he had the gall to say he was pro-school choice! He knew that school choice was a winning issue. (He was not reelected.)

I called a local political organization and was informed that in spite of his near total support for the far left agenda, he was pro-Second Amendment.

I called the NRA anyway and let them know that though he disagrees with the left on gun control, he is doing everything else to get their agenda moved forward; I gave examples of some of his lying, and said maybe this is someone they should not be endorsing. They informed me, in a business-like manner, that the NRA is a one-issue advocacy group and would continue to support him, no matter what other things he supported. I tried to explain that if enough left wingers get in, they will eventually vote as a block to rid this country of the entire Constitution. The Second Amendment will go with the rest of it, even if a small group within the left wants us to keep our guns. The girl simply kept repeating: "We're a single-issue advocacy group," and how his stand against gun control insured their support. This is not a conservative organization. Therefore, my advice is that although we all like certain individuals or organizations, do not vote for or against anyone without getting opinions from more than one source. Again, you might want to see Appendix 1 for a thumbnail list of non-establishment organizations. For state and local information, you might contact Focus on the Family to find a local organization to help you.

PLAYING THE ODDS
AND PLAYING THE EMOTIONS

People's emotions are often used to cement their position for gun control or against the right to keep and bear arms. Looking at the facts is a better way.

The main thrust of an article by Thomas Sowell that I read is that gun control advocates don't care about the facts: they start urban legends about how guns are always bad, despite overwhelming evidence to the contrary.

"Within the United States, rural areas have higher rates of gun ownership and lower rates of murder, whites have higher rates of gun ownership than blacks and much lower murder rates. For the country as a whole, handgun ownership doubled in the 20th century, while the murder rate went down. But such facts are not mentioned by gun control zealots or by the liberal media."[160]

As for the dogma that the best way to be unharmed when an intruder enters your home is non-resistance, he quotes the fact that "people who have not resisted have gotten hurt twice as often as people who resisted with a firearm."

Showing how gun controllers manipulate statistics he continues: "Most uses of guns in self-defense—whether in the home or elsewhere—do not involve actually pulling the trigger. When the intended victim turns out to have a gun in his hand, the attacker usually has enough brains to back off. But the lives saved this way do not get counted.

"People killed at home by family members are highly atypical. The great majority of these victims have had to call the police to their homes before, because of domestic violence, and

---

160 Sowell, Thomas. Commentary by Thomas Sowell; *America's First Freedom*: 32-33.

just over half have had the cops out several times. These are not just ordinary people who happened to lose their temper when a gun was at hand.

"Neither are most 'children' who are killed by guns just toddlers who happened to find a loaded weapon lying around. More of those 'children' are members of teenage criminal gangs who kill each other deliberately.

"Some small children do in fact get accidentally killed by guns in the home—but fewer than drown in bathtubs. Is anyone for banning bathtubs?"[161]

John Lott did a study of guns that showed that "gun ownership tended on net balance to reduce crime in general and murder in particular" and was published as the book, *More Guns, Less Crime*. Thomas Sowell recounts the story of how John offered a copy of the study to a leader in a gun control group, but she refused to accept it. Later the media called her to ask her opinion on the work by John and she was quoted as saying that the study was flawed. When Mr. Lott called her and asked how she came to that conclusion without reading the work, she hung up on him. (Other research of interest could be found in the books *Pointblank* by Gary Kleck and *Guns and Violence* by Joyce Lee Malcolm.)

Sowell sums up his thesis by saying, "Facts are not the real issue to gun control zealots, who typically share a general vision of the world in which their own superior wisdom and virtue need to be imposed on others, whether on guns or other things."[162] I fully concur.

One of my fondest wishes is to let everyone come to the very difficult realization that nothing is perfect and it is unreasonable to expect any facet of society can be made perfect.

The reason why this is so important is that many proponents of new systems (like gun control in the USA) try to convince us to change because we are under an imperfect system run by imperfect people. They then imply that if only we discard our present, very adequate, system and replace it with their theoretical system,

---

161 Ibid.
162 Ibid.

everything will be perfect—no one will fall between the cracks; although, this "theoretical system" has been tried many times and has had a nearly 100 percent failure rate throughout history. Actually, I know of no instance where disarming the citizenry has been a good thing.

When this regards the right to keep and bear arms, the implication is often: "If nobody has guns, no innocent people will die by guns." Or they really pull at your emotions by implying: "Especially YOUR CHILDREN will be safer if nobody has guns." Emotions are a good thing. We all have them, and we all need them. But beware of a faction that uses your own emotions to control you. We all need to think things through more thoroughly.

To give one of the most successful and extreme examples that I can think of, think about this. Over an approximately six-year period in the 1990s there were a number of school shootings. Kids got some guns and shot other kids and teachers. The cry came out from gun safety advocates that this was proof positive that we need more gun "safety" laws. But if you look at some statistics, your brain kicks in and the hysteria passes.

Even during that period, someone's chances of dying because of gun violence at a school was far, far, far less than the chance of dying an unnatural death if you were a police officer, fireman, mine worker, or convenience store clerk.

Over 40,000 people a year died in car accidents in the USA.

Even more interesting is that during this time period when 32 kids were killed in these mass school killings (the "reason" we should ban guns), 53 high school kids died playing or practicing high school football. So we should ban high school football, right? (You would have to come to this conclusion using the same logic.)

I do understand how a parent of a child killed by gun violence would want to ban guns, and how a parent of a child killed playing football could decide that football should be banned as well. But that does not mean that the rest of us must pass legislation to enforce their emotional state. More people are killed walking, driving, rock climbing, working, playing and bathing than have been killed in the same time period by school shootings. (Please let us not outlaw bathing.)

But there is a far larger question than this. Will football keep us free? It is a wonderful sport and the gladiator-like entertainment values go way back. It builds discipline, often builds character, and fosters healthy competition, if not taken to extremes. But it is not a right, and it will not keep us from becoming subjects of the state, instead of citizens of a free nation.

One of the thirteen original states went so far as to pass a law that stated that if a man were too poor to buy a gun, he could petition the state and it would buy him one. Trust me, these people were not into gun control, and they would not have written a Second Amendment that allowed gun control.

Think of the previously mentioned other countries that have tried gun control. At the time of this writing, your chances of being the victim of violent crime in London is seven times what it is in New York City.

Be aware that in most of these countries, gun registration lists were used to later confiscate those guns that were legally registered. Therefore, I must do something that I never in my life thought I would do. I must advocate that if free citizens of this country who have broken no laws related to felonies or weapons/violence charges are required to register your guns, disobey the law. The Second Amendment of the Constitution allows you to do that. Such laws are illegal under our Constitution.

"…the right of the people to keep and bear arms, shall not be infringed." This implies that registration, restrictions on law-abiding citizens carrying a gun, or special taxes on buying or selling guns would be unconstitutional. Certainly, with the potential for abuse, keeping a database of gun owners should also be unconstitutional, since such a thing could be so easily used to infringe on this right (leading to confiscation). Illinois has an unconstitutional law that requires a person to obtain a Firearms Owners Identification Card before they can buy a gun. Several states require that you sign a registration form to buy ammunition. All methods of keeping track of who owns guns include the possibility to use this information for confiscation.

In the countries listed previously almost a million guns owned by law-abiding citizens were confiscated using registration lists. Do you think those gun owners regret obeying that particular law?

I feel compelled to emphasize: Before committing totally to civil disobedience, it is important to remember that one of the things that make us Americans is that we are a nation based on law. Therefore, I recommend this: Find out what the referendum procedure in the civil unit (city, county, state or federal) that passed such a law is. Get the signatures or go through the necessary process to void those laws or get them on the next election ballot. Hopefully, you will win and disobeying the law forever will be unnecessary. If after you win, more legislators try to enact more gun control laws on law-abiding citizens, it is time for a recall election on those legislators that refuse to support the Constitution of the United States of America in regard to the Second Amendment.

Many people who read this will say, "Whoa, this is way too much trouble. It is not worth it." Unfortunately, in a country that has been free for so long, freedoms are taken for granted. Freedoms are like parents, only once they are gone will you fully appreciate them. Once those freedoms are gone, you might not have to work to get them back, you might have to die to get them back, for the good of mankind.

The following article from *World Magazine*[163] reminds us once again that before we react emotionally to rhetoric, we must look at the facts.

"Guns reduce violence, argues columnist Paul Craig Roberts, and the evidence supporting this thesis grows. He notes a new book from Joyce Lee Malcolm called *Guns and Violence*. 'When the English were armed to the teeth, violent crime was rare,' he writes. 'Now that the English are disarmed, violent crime has exploded. Indeed, crime in England is out of control.'

"Mr. Roberts also attacked the idea that guns are a constant danger to children: 'Bathtubs are twice as dangerous to children as guns. Fire is 18 times more dangerous. ...Cars are 57 times more dangerous. Household cleaners and poisons are twice as dangerous.'

---

163 Author not noted; "A Tool For Self Defense." *World Magazine*, 10 Aug 2002: 13.

"The economist also quotes statistics showing that defensive gun use stops more crimes than police intervention. 'National polls of defensive gun use by private citizens indicate that as many as 3.6 million crimes annually are prevented by armed individuals,' he pointed out. 'In 98 percent of the cases, the armed citizen merely has to brandish his weapon. As many as 400,000 people each year believe they saved a life by being armed. Contrary to Handgun Control's propaganda, in less than 1 percent of confrontations do criminals succeed in taking the gun from the intended victim.'"[164]

Many times things "seem" right because people do not think past the surface of what people are saying. For instance, every time there is a terrorist act, some unpatriotic gun control advocate in the legislature immediately introduces yet another "gun safety" law. As if this will prevent a terrorist from getting a weapon. Think about it. Whoever heard of disarming Israeli citizens because of terrorist acts? In the settlements they were encouraged to carry weapons openly because everybody knows that this discourages terrorism. All but a small handful of gun laws only serve to disarm the intended victims.

To sum it up: (1) The Constitution guarantees you have the right to own and carry a gun; (2) WE must participate in a recall election of any politician who votes to unconstitutionally relieve us of that right; (3) EVERY ONE OF US must start the drive to repeal at least one of these unconstitutional laws; (4) we must not allow ourselves to achieve victim status because we passively stood by while treasonous Americans disarmed the law-abiding citizens, including you and me.

Remember this: Any politician who votes to disarm law-abiding citizens has violated his oath to uphold the Constitution and, therefore, must be removed from office.

This would include any judge who rules in any way that violates the Second Amendment. (See my chapter "The Oligarchy of the Judiciary," which includes the importance of impeachment of judges.)

---

164 Ibid.

Chapter 11

Lost Causes

When I was a kid, I used to love watching *Casablanca* on TV. It starred Humphrey Bogart and Ingrid Bergman as well as many other greats. The scene I am about to describe was still in the movie then, but the copy I have now has it edited out, perhaps a copy cut to add more commercials.

In the scene, the evil Nazi commander is going over Rick's record of always fighting on the side of freedom seekers. He says, "It seems you are always fighting for lost causes." Rick replies, "Sometimes lost causes are the only ones worth fighting for." At the time, I was in my early to mid teens, I thought something like: "In an otherwise brilliant movie, that is the stupidest thing I have ever heard. Why throw yourself away on a lost cause? Get away, and later fight again for something you can win."

It's funny how you have to eat your own words sometimes. Many in the liberal establishment would tell me that I'm fighting for a lost cause. Just taking five examples they could show me that they are right.

1) At the time of this writing, the Shays-Meehan bill has been passed by both houses of Congress and signed into law by the President. (The Senate version is called McCain/Feingold.) This will make it a crime for many organizations that represent you and me, liberals, moderates and conservatives, to say anything about an incumbent for sixty days before a general election. It has been called the Incumbent Protection Act by those who believe in First Amendment Freedoms. And though it will silence the left and the right organizations equally, it will not silence the media. It has also been called the Media Empowerment Act. Since the media is very liberal biased, this means that the opinions of the left will be shouted from the rooftops by the media until election day, while the opinions of conservative or religious organizations and the people they represent will only be spoken by a very limited group of clearly defined organizations, and if others try to voice an opinion, they will face felony arrests, jail time and huge fines.

(And for those of you who think the 527s and the internet will help get around this, the way they did in the 2004 elections, buzz has it that Congress plans to "regulate" these more intensely in time to silence them for the 2008 elections.)

For all practical purposes, this, if not revoked, means that the First Amendment to the constitution is virtually dead, as regards the freedom of speech clause.

2) We are following in the footsteps of England in abolishing a citizens' right to bear arms. If we go just a little further, the Second Amendment dies.

3) The California legislature has expanded homosexual "rights" over the will of the people, per prior referendum vote. Some say that as California goes, so goes the rest of the nation.

4) People by the millions have been successfully brainwashed into believing God in general and Christianity in specific must be outlawed in all public arenas.

5) During 2004, the Senate Judiciary Committee refused to let any Bush nominee to the federal bench have a full Senate hearing if the nominee is pro-life, conservative, or Christian. So much for the left's dedication to diversity!

These five factors, and others, lead me to feel, sometimes, that I am fighting for a lost cause. Think about it. I believe that the four social ills outlined in this book, left unchecked, will destroy America. To summarize, they are: (A) ripping out America's Christian foundation; (B) replacing capitalism with socialism; (C) discontinuing our uniquely American culture; and (D) implementation of the homosexual agenda.

I only started writing this book after I felt all of these goals of the left were more than half accomplished. I have no natural powers of persuasion, yet this book has to convince the majority of moderates to come to my point of view on crucial issues to save the USA. And hundreds of thousands of those moderates, as well as many conservatives, must become more politically active to win this greatest of all wars.

Am I fighting for a lost cause? It doesn't matter because compared to the alternatives it is the only cause worth fighting for.

If we lose our American culture, we lose our honesty and integrity; if we become socialist, we lose our wealth, and thereafter, our power; if the homosexual agenda is installed, we lose our children and grandchildren; if we lose our Christian foundation, we lose our freedom. This four-pronged pincer movement has gained so much power, such an unbelievable amount of inertia, that without participation of the hitherto silent majority of Americans, this may be our American Waterloo.

Ironically, it might be neither the left nor the right who will determine the future of this country. It will take the active involvement of that largest segment of our society, the moderates, to save the day. A good rule of thumb would be: If a law, politician or judge violates the Bill of Rights (the first ten amendments to the Constitution) fight to get rid of them at all costs. If the moderates continue to do nothing, the greatest country in the world will pass into history. If they get motivated and fight for the kind of ideals they are reading about in this book, the greatest experiment in freedom the world has ever known will continue.

TO BE SPECIFIC

It is hard to overemphasize the importance of all Americans' need to realize the brainwashing perpetrated by the left-leaning bias of the major media. A great example is the infamous Murphy Brown speech by Dan Quayle. Remember what a fool the late night comedians made of Quayle? For months the media castigated the man for such an idiotic speech. He was a real moron for saying such things if all you knew was what the media said about it. Or was he? Pay particular attention to the quotation marks in the next few pages; they are excerpts from the "Murphy Brown" speech. [AKA "Address to the Commonwealth Club of California."]

In rereading the speech, the first several pages mention such things as: (1) High-ranking officials of other countries asking him why the riots occurred in LA after the Rodney King verdict. (2) "What happened? Why? And how do we prevent it in the future?" (3) "Who is to blame for the riots? The rioters are to blame. Who is to blame for the killings? The killers are to blame. Yes, I can understand how people were shocked and outraged by the verdict in the Rodney King trial. But there is simply no excuse for the mayhem that followed. To apologize or in any way to excuse what happened is wrong. It is a betrayal of all those people equally outraged and equally disadvantaged who did not loot and did not riot—and who were in many cases victims of the rioters...the riots were wrong. And if we as a society don't condemn what is wrong, how can we teach our children what is right?" (4) "I believe the lawless social anarchy which we saw is directly related to the breakdown of family structure, personal responsibility and social order in too many areas of our society." (5) He goes on to mention our progress: abolition of slavery in the 1860s and the end of segregation and other civil rights advances of the 1960s. "Since 1967 the median income of black two-parent families has risen by 60 percent in real terms.... The number of black college graduates has skyrocketed.... black mayors head 48 of our largest cities." (6) "But as we all know, there is another side to that bright landscape....We have also developed a culture of poverty—some call it an underclass—that is far more violent and harder to escape than it was a generation ago." "...poverty has traditionally been a stage through which people pass on their way to joining the great middle class. And if one generation didn't get very far up the ladder—their ambitious, better-educated children would.

"But the underclass seems to be a new phenomenon. It is a group whose members are dependent on welfare for very long stretches, and whose men are often drawn into lives of crime. There is far too little upward mobility, because the underclass is disconnected from the rules of American society. And these problems have, unfortunately, been particularly acute for black Americans."

- In 1967 68 percent of black families were headed by married couples. In 1991, only 48 percent of black families were headed by both a husband and wife.
- In 1965 the illegitimacy rate among black families was 28 percent. In 1989, 65 percent—two-thirds—of all black children were born to never-married mothers.
- In 1951 9.2 percent of black youth between sixteen and nineteen were unemployed. By 1989, the number was 32 percent.
- The leading cause of death of young black males today is homicide.

"…we are in large measure reaping the whirlwind of decades of changes in social mores."

"…let's look at one unfortunate legacy of the 'Boomer' generation. When we were young, it was fashionable to declare war against traditional values. Indulgence and self-gratification seemed to have no consequences. Many of our generation glamorized casual sex and drug use, evaded responsibility and trashed authority. …The responsibility of having families has helped many recover traditional values. …But many of the poor, with less to fall back on, did not."

He goes on to talk about poverty, gangs, drive-by shootings, lack of safety in the ghetto, etc.

"When families fail, society fails. The anarchy and lack of structure in our inner cities are testament to how quickly civilization falls apart when the family foundation cracks. Children need love and discipline. They need mothers and fathers. A welfare check is not a husband. The state is not a father. It is from parents that children learn how to behave in society…."

"And for those concerned about children growing up in poverty, we should know this: marriage is probably the best anti-poverty program of all. Among families headed by married couples today, there is a poverty rate of 5.7%. But 33.4% of families headed by a single mother are in poverty today."

"Nature abhors a vacuum. Where there are no mature, responsible men around to teach boys how to be good men, gangs serve in their place. In fact, gangs have become a surrogate family for much of a generation of inner-city boys."

"...Answers to our problems won't be easy.

"We can start by dismantling a welfare system that encourages dependency and subsidizes broken families. We can attach conditions—such as school attendance, or work—to welfare. We can limit the time a recipient gets benefits. We can stop penalizing marriage for welfare mothers. We can enforce child support payments.

"Ultimately, however, marriage is a moral issue that requires cultural consensus, and the use of social sanctions. Bearing babies irresponsibly is, simply, wrong. Failing to support children one has fathered is wrong. We must be unequivocal about this.

"It doesn't help matters when prime time TV has Murphy Brown—a character who supposedly epitomizes today's intelligent, highly paid, professional woman—mocking the importance of fathers, by bearing a child alone, and calling it just another 'lifestyle choice.'

"I know it is not fashionable to talk about moral values, but we need to do it. Even though our cultural leaders in Hollywood, network TV, the national newspapers routinely jeer at them, I think that most of us in this room know that some things are good, and other things are wrong. Now it's time to make the discussion public."[165]

As most of you remember, the major media's way of public discussion was simply to "jeer" and make fun of Dan Quayle for daring to say things like, "Two parents, married to each other, are better in most cases for children than one."

---

165 Quayle, Dan. *Standing Firm.* "Address to the commonwealth Club of California, May 19, 1992": HarperCollins Publishers, 1994

Now if the media made Quayle look like a fool when what he really said was quite brilliant and was among the things that led to the welfare reform of the 1990s, can you understand how many wrong roads the bias of the establishment media leads you down?

As for why the major media did this to Quayle, I have my own personal hypothesis: The liberal media saw their champion, liberal president Carter, swept out of office by a conservative, Ronald Reagan. It became obvious that his vice president, George Bush, fairly conservative, was going to replace him. I believe that the media went hysterical with the fear that the country was going to have a virtual dynasty of conservative presidents. Among other things, this would eventually mean replacing liberal activist federal judges who legislate from the bench with conservative justices who only interpret the law in accordance with the Constitution. This is just an example of the "horrible" things that might happen if the "conservative dynasty" did get established.

Therefore, the liberal media decided that whoever Bush chose as a vice president, unless he was a true liberal, he must be attacked, humiliated, laughed at and, politically, destroyed. And to our shame, the American people bought it.

Let's face it, hundreds, if not thousands, of the best investigative reporters in the world did everything at their disposal to discredit Dan Quayle and if you look past the rhetoric, the real dirt they dug up on the guy was this (and this is the worst they could find) (1) He had belonged to the National Guard, (2) he believed a cue card written by an educator that misspelled "potato," (3) he believes that, on average, two-parent families are better for children than single-parent families. And for this, the media stirred up the public to run him out of town. And they're doing the same sort of thing to you right now on many other subjects, or about many other people. That is why I list in Appendix 1 a few of the non-establishment (today's equivalent of the old 'underground') publications. This is so you can have the chance to get some information that is not totally liberal biased.

Since the liberal establishment is so good at propaganda that it can make a good man, an honorable man, look like a buffoon, should we just give up? Is it a lost cause? The answer is up to us. If we get involved, together we can save America.

I was watching the film version of *The Lord of the Rings, The Two Towers.* As the Orc armies advanced on Theoden's kingdom, I thought him a fool and a coward to refuse Strider's request that they go out and meet the enemy head on. Instead the king chose to retreat to Helms Deep, a mighty fortress in which to hide. But now instead of rallying thousands to meet the enemy head on in the field, only three hundred defended the Deep against ten thousand Orcs. J.R.R. Tolkien said that *The Lord of the Rings* was just a story, no symbolism was meant by it. And yet he had seen his fellow Christians in his beloved England retreat from an ever-growing tide of humanism and secularism, retreating to the safety of their churches, ceding politics and public debate to those who want never to hear from Christendom again. Church attendance dropped as salvation in Jesus Christ seemed to become irrelevant as its influence on society lessened. We are about fifty years behind England, but now we are at a crossroads where we may catch up. At the climatic scene of the movie, the vast Orc army is starting to overwhelm the Castle—they are streaming through the gate, a breach in the wall, over the walls with ladders, it seems hopeless. The defenders mount up to finally do an offensive charge! As they charge, a huge army, led by Gandolf, comes to the rescue. The Orcs lose the battle after all.

In my symbolism, both the Orcs and the rescuers represent moderates and nominal Christians in America. If conservatives and Bible-believing Christians influence them, they become the rescuers. If liberals and Christ-haters lead them or they chose to do nothing, they become Orcs.

So good King Theoden simply did what American Christians did the first thirty years of the liberal takeover. At the time of this writing the Orcs are storming Helms Deep. The point of this book is simply to give US citizens enough information to let them be able to come to the conclusion that they would rather be rescuers of our society rather than destroyers of it. And the way it has worked, if you don't take a side, the Orcs win.

THE PROPAGANDA MINISTRY/FRONT

This is a facet that often seems so overwhelming. From the late 1960s until the early 1990s, the left had a virtual monopoly on the media. For 25 years you could not get information that did not go through a liberal filter unless you made a concerted effort to find an obscure source. Thus the media became a liberal propaganda machine. Yet, they constantly referred to freedom of speech and diversity. Then, Rush Limbaugh became a conservative national voice. These believers in diversity, liberals, immediately tried to pass legislation in the halls of Congress that got nicknamed the "Crush Rush" bill. They tried to legislate him out of business for disagreeing with the liberal establishment. Luckily, a large enough portion of the US population had gotten sick of the hypocrisy and voted in a slightly conservative Congress that got power in the early 1990s and ended this irrational attempt to end free speech in America.

One of the mantras that are repeated endlessly in one form or another states the liberal belief that anytime you write a view opposing theirs, you are telling your readers to kill members of that liberal group. This totally bewilders me. I've never met any of these potential murderers, nor have I heard of them except from the left, so I have extreme doubts that there are that many out there. For instance: Mathew Sheppard was murdered by two thugs and many on the left said they were motivated to do so because Focus on the Family had advertised that leaving the homosexual lifestyle was an attainable goal. Do YOU see a direct connection there? To many on the left it is obvious. To those of us in the real world, that is an extremely far stretch. But maybe what it really is is something they do not believe either, but it is just propaganda.

One of the forms of propaganda is in the use of exaggeration. When secularists compare Christians to Islamic jihadists time and again, it starts to feel somewhat OK. But analysis shows the absurdity of such concepts:

"According to this way of thinking, which has become commonplace in academia, evangelicals and jihadists are essentially the same. They both oppose homosexuality (as if opposing gay marriage were the same thing as stoning homosexuals to death.) They are both 'anti-women' (with opposition to abortion as the moral equivalent of the utter subjugation of women in Muslim countries).... Fundamentalists of both sides are violent, murderous, and oppressive (with the war against terrorism as the moral equivalent of terrorism itself.)

"Such paranoia, ignorance, and lack of any sense of proportion is laughable, of course, but it represents a new phase of anti-Christian bigotry."[166]

Add to this the screaming about creating a theocracy every time anyone with religious values runs for office or supports anyone running for office and you understand how what should be considered excessive exaggeration is commonly used.

Moving on to a more recent example of the power of the propaganda machine is its influence on minorities. Most minorities vote for liberal Democrats. Liberal Democrats block the advancement of minorities such as in the case of President Bush's nomination of Miguel Estrada to the federal court of appeals in the District of Columbia.

Also, the liberal Democrats block school choice initiatives such as school voucher programs. Cal Thomas puts it this way: "It is more than irony that Republicans are the staunchest backers of school choice when the beneficiaries are primarily minority children whose parents mostly vote for Democrats, and Democrats oppose it in the face of overwhelming approval among one of their biggest constituencies."[167] Thus is the power of the propaganda wars that succeed in winning votes from minorities to support liberal Democrats that turn around and do things that prevent minorities from gaining better education and, eventually, more power.

---

166 Veith, Gene Edward. "Taliban west?" *World Magazine* 25 Dec. 2004: 24.
167 Cal Thomas. "Desperate times" *World Magazine* 31 May 2003: 24.

Our system was designed so that the majority would not tyrannize the minorities (and I do not just mean racial minorities), but the ACLU and other leftist groups have redesigned it so the majority is often tyrannized by the minorities. Whether you are talking about forcing private organizations that believe homosexuality is wrong to hire gays, or private women's clubs to accept men as members or universities to pass over more qualified candidates to admit less qualified people because of the color of their skin, it is still a dictatorship of the minority status. Taking away one group's freedom of choice to give a different group hegemony over them is not right, but it is being done more and more in western civilization.

THE SIGN OF OUR TIMES

June 26, 2003 will be another day that will live in infamy. The US Supreme Court ruled in (*Lawrence vs Texas*) that the Texas law which made sodomy illegal was unconstitutional. Talk about opening the floodgates. According to what I hope are pessimistic commentators, this ruling will result in the total accomplishment of the rest of the homosexual agenda as outlined in the Gay Rights Platform of 1972. Domestic partner benefits and civil unions will become gay marriage; a few states allowing gay adoption will become universal; California's ever-expanding of "gay rights" will probably soon include teaching it in the schools; it will become illegal to quote the Bible or mention morality in regard to homosexuality, and if you do, you will be jailed or fined into poverty.

When the Supreme Court of the United States of America decides that the outlawing of moral deviancy is unconstitutional, this could be the beginning of the end of us. The progress of the implementation of the homosexual agenda is accelerating so fast that when I started writing this book, that agenda was little more than a brief mention. Now it is one of my biggest and most important chapters. How we have regressed so far, so quickly is beyond all logical reasoning.

So, what do you think? Am I fighting for a lost cause? Will you join me?

If you are a conservative Democrat, get involved in the party, become a precinct committeeman, or find another way to voice your opinion in the party. If you are a moderate, stop voting for the liberals that will eventually take away all the power from all the people, including you. Find sources that are not liberal biased, so you can hear both sides of the cultural struggle. A few are listed among those listed in Appendix 1. If you are a liberal, open your mind to the possibility that what you have been told to believe could be wrong. The continued greatness of America depends on it.

Chapter 12

A War on All Fronts

THE TWILIGHT OF CAMELOT

In the United States of America, our traditional, Western, Judeo-Christian culture is collapsing. It is not collapsing because it failed. On the contrary, it has given us the freest and most prosperous society in human history. Rather, it is collapsing because we are abandoning it. Starting in the mid-1960s, we have thrown away the values, morals, and standards that define traditional Western culture. In part, this has been driven by cultural radicals, people who hate our Judeo-Christian culture. Dominant in the elite, especially in the universities, the media, and the entertainment industry, the cultural radicals have successfully pushed an agenda of moral relativism, militant secularism, and sexual and social 'liberation.'"[168]

The United States of America has achieved more individual freedom, personal and collective wealth, and national power than has ever been dreamed of in the world prior to this. This

---

168 William S. Lind, et. Al; *Marine Corps Gazette*, Dec. 1994: Pg. 37.

has been Camelot. Not that we have solved all our problems, but the problems have been smaller and more easily solvable than in most other countries.

This could be the twilight of Camelot since liberalism has made such incredible strides in replacing those supporting beams that have made our country what it is today. The results of their agenda so far have been, in part:

1) An ever-growing governmental system, increasing in control over the people's lives, draining their wealth through unnecessary taxes to support programs that the Constitution does not authorize.
2) More and more socialism, people growing ever more dependant on the government for sustenance and direction; accompanied by an ever diminishing sense of self-reliance.
3) More women and children in poverty due to the change in social mores.
4) A sexually transmitted disease epidemic, including a million people with AIDS.
5) Over forty million American babies aborted in the first thirty years after *Roe v. Wade.*
   A) Leading to a much smaller working force in the future to support aging baby boomers on Social Security and other pension plans.
   B) Leading to a culture of death, which will probably lead to the termination of the elderly and infirm in the near future, whether they agree they are ready to go or not.
   C) Which has had the psychological effect of lessening the perceived value of life, which may be partly responsible for the increase in child abuse.
   D) A smaller growth factor, slowing economic growth.
6) Unilateral disarmament during years when liberals are in control of the federal government, making us more vulnerable and less capable of action when needed.

This is just the war on the liberal political front. Then we have terrorists and international enemies who are just waiting for us to lose our wealth and power, so they can erode us away so we will at least be totally ineffective if not conquerable. Think of what someone like Saddam Hussein would have been able to do if the US had been unable to stop him in 1991. The entire Middle East might have fallen to him. Once in charge of so much of the world's oil, after consolidating his base and increasing his infrastructure, he or his successor then could move on to conquering the Balkans in one direction or India in the other.

Is this a far-fetched scenario? Without our influence the world would be a very different and much more dismal place. Stories that were once fodder for B grade science fiction movies and apocalyptic novels could easily become the new reality.

THE MEDIA

Many years ago it seemed to me that the media was drifting further and further to the left. Finally, it was so obvious that I thought of a paradigm to test the hypothesis that the media is biased to the left using the old *extrapo ad absurdum* (extrapolate to absurdity) used in some forms of mathematical analysis.

You simply extrapolate and exaggerate your parameters (P) and see what conclusions you can draw from them.

P1: Presume that all promoting and hiring in 1952 had been such that all the management and top level executives in the media were conservatives.

P2: Assume that the workers who might be hired or promoted were 50 percent conservative and 50 percent of them were liberal.

P3: Conservatives, being fair minded and more open minded than liberals, hire and promote based on an individual's abilities.

P4: Liberals, being less open minded and much more dogmatic, hire and promote based on the worker's agreement with their own world view.

P5: Presume liberals and conservatives are statistically equal in abilities, and therefore, should get hired/promoted in equal numbers (at least if hiring/promoting is done in a strictly unbiased manner.)

P6: Presume that a generation of hiring/promoting in the media is a ten-year cycle. This would mean that every ten years you have a "generation" of new hires; every ten years you have a new "generation" of supervisors/executives.

Using these parameters, from 1952 to 1962 the makeup of the media would have gone from 100 percent conservative to 50 percent conservative, 50 percent liberal. From 1962 to 1972 it would have gone from 50/50 to 25 percent conservative, 75 percent liberal. By 1992 the media would be 93 3/4 percent liberal, 6 1/4 percent conservative. In 1992 89 percent of the media voted for Bill Clinton as president.

Now I understand that many moderates reading this are going to say, "Wait a minute, I'm a moderate and I voted for him too." True. But ask yourself this: Are you actively pursuing a career for the rest of your life that will enable you to "change the world"? For the majority of us on planet Earth, the answer would be no. The reason I asked the question is because in a recent survey when journalism students were asked why they chose the profession of journalism, the most common answer was, "Because I want to change the world." Perhaps I could be wrong, but I don't think that is the response of a moderate. Although I have to add that most moderates are good people and most good people want to leave the world a little better by the time they leave than it was when they got here, but that is not the same as "I want to change the world."

"I want to change the world" would be said by, more likely, a leader or at least an activist. Besides journalists, look at how many Hollywood stars, movie and TV stars, are politically active, going to other countries on political missions like Bono to Africa or Sean Penn to Baghdad.

Barbra Streisand called together Democratic leaders like Tom Daschle and met with them to discuss battle plans. Sometimes during the year it seems like they all get some press time discussing politics and their individual opinion of what politician is great or which one, if elected, would cause them to leave the country: the point being that leaders and activists are usually either conservatives or liberals. Activists are rarely moderates.

Therefore, if 89 percent of the media is liberal (as of 1992), there is no way my parameters can be absurd, since they got an answer within 5 percent of reality. This implies that there has been active discrimination and bigotry in reference to hiring and promoting of conservatives in the media. Of course, the obvious liberal bias in the media makes this axiomatic, but I just hadn't previously realized that it was mathematically provable.

As I grew older, I became more and more aware of the world situations and one of the sayings I came up with was: "There is a word for Christians and conservatives in Hollywood; it's 'unemployed.' " It's like these people cheat, but there is no referee to make them obey civilized rules. Is there no redress for this? Some say, "Conservatives could start their own major movie studio." That would cost a couple billion dollars; and after fifty years of discrimination in hiring, how many conservatives have the training and experience to run the hundreds of different jobs in a studio, even if they had the money? It would seem that the best way to right this wrong would be to get the liberals to regain their sense of fair play. To stop labeling every conservative as a "far right extremist" and to realize that it is just not right to make certain that anybody who doesn't agree with your world view is further labeled unemployable. Maybe with the influx of fresh ideas from conservatives, for example, all the sitcoms would stop looking alike—the same promotion of abortion, sex outside of marriage, homosexuality, liberal politics mixed with the denigration of marriage, traditional American culture, and Christianity. A few of them are brilliantly written, but it's like listening to a wonderfully crafted piece of music meant to be done by an entire orchestra, but you are only allowed to hear the part done by one instrument.

If you don't hire any blacks, it's obvious that you're a bigot if there are plenty of blacks around that are qualified to do the job and you have lots of employees...all white. But you cannot file a class action suit about not hiring enough conservatives. We come in all sizes, shapes and colors, not to mention both sexes.

By now, some of you are asking: "Where did this constant march toward the left in the media come from?" I have a hypothesis on that.

It dates back to the "McCarthy era" in the early 1950s. It is one of the blackest periods in our country's history.

The House Un-American Activities Committee was looking for communists. They practiced unconstitutional persecution of suspected communists. They absolutely shredded the Constitution and got away with it. Understanding the propaganda power of the entertainment industry, and using its fame and glamour to insure massive media coverage, its fiercest attacks were against the movie industry. After interrogating, humiliating, and blacklisting several people in Hollywood, destroying their reputations, ruining their careers and making all the people in that field feel completely helpless, this committee had accidentally done more to stimulate the complete takeover of the media by the left than anyone else ever has. The unintended consequence of this modern-day witch hunt was that the left-leaning elements in the media were terrified and full of hatred for anyone and anything that seemed right of center, or even not far left enough to suit them. I believe it was this "anti-McCarthyism backlash" that has led to the attitudes that made the above statistical analysis so accurate.

I just wish that someone who was actively involved in film making during the backlash takeover; someone who was discriminated against, someone like Charlton Heston or Gail Davis, would do the research, interview the few remaining people who saw this happen, and write their own book on this subject. By the early 1970s a fifteen-year president of a major studio was giving a lecture on a college campus. When mentioning this subject he said:

"People ask me what's going on in Hollywood.... I don't know. A new guy, Robert Deniro makes two pictures and he can suddenly pick any film he wants to star in, name his own salary, do anything he wants. After TWO pictures!! Meanwhile Charlton Heston can't get arrested in this town."

The ironic thing is that Hollywood harps on the horrible inequities of the McCarthy era as exemplified by the blacklisting (making it so certain people couldn't work in Hollywood anymore), particularly the "Hollywood 10." Yet, now that the left is in charge, they have blacklisted at least a thousand times as many people as the Hollywood Ten. Instead of a specific list of particular names, it is simply a commonly understood group that is actually quite large that is blacklisted—anyone who doesn't agree with the liberal worldview. In other words, the bigotry is against anyone who is pro-life, is tolerant of Bible-believing Christians, anyone who is more capitalist than socialist or does not 100 percent support the gay rights platform of 1972, or believes that the government should not be in charge of every aspect of its citizens lives (with the exception of the rich and powerful liberals themselves), and, especially, you cannot believe in the U.S. Constitution as it was written (with all those pesky individual rights in the first ten amendments.)

Mr. David Horowitz, the radical 1960s leftist who became a conservative, summarized the left in this country best when he said: "There's nothing liberal about the left except on two issues: Personal sex activity and personal drug use. On everything else they are totalitarians."

Coincidently, most of the things that Hollywood is against virtually define traditional American culture. Americanism is a rugged individualism, where hard work is rewarded, sloth goes unrewarded and people are free to believe what they want, even if it is politically incorrect.

To give another example of the left bias of the media: They hate the fact that George W. Bush became president instead of Al Gore. A horrible conservative got the job instead of a wonderful liberal. In *Time Magazine* dated March 24, 2003, "Memories from Right Now," page 8, author unlisted, it states: "Bush, loser of the popular vote, won the Presidency in electoral votes by fiat of the Supreme Court." According to Funk & Wagnalls Standard College Dictionary: FIAT: "A positive and authoritative order or decree." This implies that Florida (via their State Supreme Court) had ruled properly, going down a road that would make sure that Gore won, but the US Supreme Court simply ordered Bush the winner. This is two years after we knew that exactly the opposite was true.

Florida election law states: "Deadline returns must be filed by 5 P.M. on the 7th day following the...general election." (Section 102.112). By that deadline, the tally showed Bush the winner. The Florida Supreme Court kept illegally ordering an extension of the deadline and one recount after another, hoping that if the votes were recounted enough times, one would come out Gore the winner and then they could stop recounting. This was very likely since the Florida Justices were Democrats and ordered the recounts in only Democratic majority counties.

In short order, the case reached the US Supreme Court, who turned it back with the implication: please look at the law and make a decision based on the law. The Florida Supreme court implied back: What? We get to decide! Screw the law! Keep counting until Gore wins. That was when the US Supreme Court finally forced the Florida Supreme Court to obey the law. Over two years later, *Time Magazine* is still coming right out and saying that the opposite of what really happened is true.

SNAPSHOTS OF MEDIA BIAS[169]

In his newsletter, Rush Limbaugh gives many examples of media bias. (1) In Bosnia, Clinton promised troops would be home by Christmas 1997. In 2003, they were still there. No media complaints. Before Bush sent troops to Iraq, the media was crying, "Where's the exit strategy?" (2) When Schwarzenegger ran for governor of California, he was beaten mercilessly by the media for sexual improprieties that occurred decades before; and this, not even because they disagree with his liberal views, but simply because he claims to be a Republican. Yet when Clinton had even worse misbehavior far more recently, the media (and other liberals) decried: "Hey, it's his private life! It doesn't affect the way he does his job!" (3)When George W. Bush refused federal matching funds that cap spending he was assaulted by the

---

169 From: Limbaugh, Rush. "Double Standard" *The Limbaugh Letter* Nov.2003; 14.

media's charges of being a rich, spoiled elitist. Years later, when Howard Dean did the same thing, the media response was a pat on the back to him.

(4) When Newt Gingrich accepted a $4.5 million book advance, the media hounded him until he agreed not to accept the money until after the book sold. Yet, a few years later, when Hillary Clinton got an $8 million book advance, the media just said she was "shrewd." All you need is a little discernment and an average memory to see the overwhelmingly liberal bias in the media.

THE IMPORTANCE OF FAMILY

In this war for the heart and soul and even the very life of America, you can be a true hero. No, I'm not talking about the kind of hero that makes points on a professional sports team; I am talking about the kind of heroes that gave their lives to make America free. You won't have to die, but you will have to make sacrifices. You and millions of others like you, no matter which you are, conservative, liberal, moderate or other, can be absolutely instrumental in saving America.

But many will not like this. For some it will be the greatest sacrifice you ever made.

In every social class, every income bracket, every region of the country, we have lost battle after battle to America's detriment. The enemy is divorce. We are talking about fathering children with women or girls you are not married to. On average, a third of our children do not know what it would have been like to grow up with both their natural parents fully involved in their lives, living under the same roof. This is destroying our next generation of Americans.

"...children growing up without a married mother and father are about twice as likely to drop out of school, over 50 percent more likely to have a child themselves as a teenager, and over 50 percent more likely to abuse drugs or alcohol."[170]

---

170 Graham, Tim. "First comes reform, then comes marriage" *World Magazine.* 16 Mar 2002: 20.

In the same article it went on to state: "The greatest unintended consequence of the 'War on Poverty' was family breakdown." (We rewarded people for not marrying or having more children out of wedlock.) "Overall, out-of-wedlock births rose from 8 percent of all births in 1965 to an astonishing 33 percent in 1994."[171]

Allowing ourselves to be fooled into thinking that staying together in marriage is not very important has led to tremendous consequences.

"Seventy percent of African-American babies and 19 percent of white babies in the United States are born out of wedlock. Most will never know their fathers or experience what it means to be loved by them. Only 34 percent of all children born in America will live with both biological parents through age eighteen. This is a recipe for trouble, especially when we consider the fact that 62 percent of mothers with children under three are employed. The number was half that in 1975! Fully 72 percent of mothers with children under eighteen currently hold jobs."[172]

The statistics are in and all our excuses about why it was better for the kids that we got divorced have been shown to be hogwash. The sexual revolution of the 1960s may have convinced us that sex is just good, clean fun and there is no need for commitment; but that is one of the many ideas of that time that research has since shown to be totally false.

I could go into details about the severe increase in women and children in poverty, the emotional destruction of the deserted parent and the children, the tragedy of millions of abortions and the post-abortion syndrome thereafter. But what is really important is that we are destroying the next generation of Americans by not giving them the security of the two-parent families that is their right to expect.

Sex was never meant to be a substitute for love. Sex was meant to be a symbol of the commitment of love. I'm probably

---

171 Ibid.
172 Dobson, Dr. James. "Family News from Dr. James Dobson." March 2002. 2.

about to fight for another one of my lost causes, but in this facet of life, it is the only one worth fighting for.

Guys, if you are not fully committed to spending the rest of your life with a woman, you should not be screwing her…and if you are not married to her that is all you are doing. After the wedding you will truly be making love to her, because love is about commitment.

Girls, if you are having sex with a guy because he will not wait until the wedding night, or worse, he has not even started to think about marriage; or worse yet, if that is the only way to keep him, then maybe he is not worth keeping.

Don't get me wrong. Sex is more valuable than gold, but do you know anybody who gives gold away? You pay dollars for gold, but sex is so much more valuable that you should have to pay for it with commitment.

In this instance, what I am really talking about is what this all means to the next generation. Our free-love attitude has totally screwed up many of the children. More juvenile crime, more violence, more prison inmates, more people going through life hurting and going down all the wrong paths. For a thorough analysis read *Bringing Up Boys* by Dr. James Dobson. We are sacrificing our children on the twin altar of living totally for self and lack of commitment.

Let me give two examples of what lack of commitment leads to: (1) A new girl came to work and I was assigned to train her. During the many hours we spent together I learned significant things about her personally. She was twenty-four years old, had four children by at least three different guys and had never been married. Now, she was a tall, exotic beauty with a dynamite fig-ure. I perfectly understand why most any man would have the impulse to want to have sex with her. But because of this lack of judgment on her part and lack of commitment on the guys' parts, she is having to work full time to support four kids by herself, her mother is having to raise the kids while she is at work, and the children have no father figure to build in that facet of respect for authority and other fatherly benefits. This is both tragic to her and a dangerous consequence to society. (2)

My daughter started a new friendship with a girl—let's call her Juliet—when they were in the seventh grade. At first it was just another little friend, another little girl in my mind. Then when I found out her family history, I took a second look from a different point of view and came to the conclusion that this girl is headed for trouble. Her father was married to his third wife. They were raising five kids. Three were half-siblings to each other and two were unrelated to those, but half-siblings to each other. Juliet's mother lived in another state. She was raising four kids by I don't know how many men. Juliet's mom is a single mother. I found out from my daughter that Juliet's mom had had the sex conversation with Juliet, and advised her to hold off on having sex until she was sixteen! In other words, look at how we, your parents, have screwed up our lives, now you go out and make the same mistakes yourself! Then I looked at Juliet in a way that I almost never let myself look at girls under eighteen years of age. She was about five inches taller than my daughter of the same age. She needed a little filling in, but not much; and she was pretty. She was fourteen. By the time she is sixteen, she will virtually be a lightning rod to boys. And her mother just gave her permission to become sexually active at that time—another life of tragedy and hardship in the making.

Next time you are thinking of having sex with a new partner realize that it REALLY means (1) I want to spend the rest of my life with this person. No matter what, I will stay with him or her. (2) The kids that may come of this are my responsibility until they are adults. Correction: Our responsibility together.

Even though this is not one of my four main contentions in this book on how America is being destroyed, and how to prevent that destruction, in my reading I became aware that we could reverse all four of the other pillars' destruction and yet one of the unintended consequences of our hedonism that leads to pre-marital sex, extramarital sex, and divorce, could be that America is destroyed anyway.

The family is the framework of our house (society). Destroy the framework and the house falls. There are so many reasons to split up. (1) He's a loser; (2) she's asexual; (3) he gets violent; (4) she never wants to do what I want to do; (5) They have an addiction; (6) My partner is irresponsible; etc., ad infinitum. If it is really that bad, get help!

I sincerely doubt that there is anybody who has been married a significant amount of time who has not thought they would be better off with someone else, or even with nobody at all. But as bad as it gets, you owe it to your children to work it through. You can consider it the price you need to pay to keep this country free, strong, healthy and wealthy. **YOU, no matter how poor, tired and frustrated you are, really are that important!** When we don't get help, when we don't learn to compromise or see the other person's side, when we make life intolerable for our partners, when we and our partners get one step closer to splitting up, we are putting another nail in the coffin of America. Everyone also has to learn that there are a few things that will never change in our partners and we just have to live with those traits. **This may be the only opportunity in your life to be a true hero.** You can do it if you try. You can stay together and overcome the problems because you are an American, because you don't give up, because the kids are important to you—it does not matter why we do it, just so we do it. I know there are exceptions, perhaps a total psychopath who cannot stop beating his wife; or a partner who compulsively cheats on their spouse. But the problem is that we *all* think *our* situation is the exception! Or we don't have the guts to stand up, tell the person what is wrong and force ourselves into both seeking help. It is easier to run, get out.

One reason for breakups is that it takes most new couples five to ten years to understand that there are often major issues that there can be no compromise on and we simply have to learn to live with that trait of the other person. Since many divorces occur before the marriage is that old, they did not have the chance to learn this, accept it, and learn to live with it. So then they start the cycle all over again.

In a study by the Institute for American Values in New York, it was found that "Among those who initially rated their marriages as 'very unhappy,' but remained together, nearly 80 percent considered themselves 'happily married and 'much happier' five years later. ...only 19 percent of those who got divorced or separated were happy five years later."[173]

"Prisons are populated primarily by men who were abandoned or rejected by their fathers. Motivational speaker and writer Zig Ziglar quotes his friend Bill Glass, a dedicated evangelist who counseled almost every weekend for twenty-five years with men who were incarcerated, as saying that among the thousands of prisoners he had met, not one of them genuinely loved his dad. Ninety-five percent of those on death row hated their fathers."[174] To further exemplify the importance of staying together for the children, Dr. Dobson goes on to state: "Some years ago, executives of a greeting-card company decided to do something special for Mother's Day. They set up a table in a federal prison, inviting any inmate who so desired to send a free card to his mom. The lines were so long, they had to make another trip to the factory to get more cards. Due to the success of the event, they decided to do the same thing on Father's Day, but this time no one came. Not one prisoner felt the need to send a card to his dad. Many had no idea who their fathers even were." (James Robison, *My Father's Face: A Portrait of the Perfect Father*; Sisters, OR: Multnomah Press, 1997.) What a sobering illustration of a dad's importance to his children."[175]

CITIZENSHIP

When I was in high school in the mid 1960s, one of my teachers tried to explain how complicated international laws on the birthright of citizenship were. He gave the example that if you were an American couple on a British airline flying over France and the woman gave birth right then, the child would be a citizen of all three countries until their eighteenth birthday, at which time they would have to pick one to be a citizen of.

---

173 Dobson, Dr. James. Family News From Dr. James Dobson Sept 2002: 1
174 Dobson, Dr. James. Family News From Dr. James Dobson Mar 2002: 4 & 5.
175 Ibid.

As the gulf between rich countries and poor countries widened, most major nations had the problem of pregnant women who were illegal aliens smuggling into their country just to have their baby, so it would be a citizen of the rich nation and she and her spouse could live there to take care of their child. When the trickle became a flood, every major nation changed their law so under any of the above circumstances, the kid will not be a citizen of the nation if the kid is the child of illegal immigrants.

The United States remains the only wealthy nation that allows thousands of illegal aliens to continue to abuse this policy and get around the other limitations on immigration.

The reason for this is that in other countries it was merely a change in their immigration laws: quite simple. But with us it is in the Fourteenth Amendment to our Constitution. Section I: "All persons <u>born</u> or naturalized in the United States and subject to the jurisdiction thereof are citizens of the United States and of the State wherein they reside…." We need to change it to: "All persons born or naturalized in the United States, except the children of illegal aliens, and subject to the jurisdiction thereof are citizens of the United States and of the State wherein they reside…." and then keep the rest of the meaning of the amendment in. We have to quit rewarding lawbreakers!

Some will say that you can't do that. It will require a Constitutional Convention and then the whole Constitution can be changed. This is not necessarily true. In 1970-1971 the Twenty-Sixth Amendment was added (changing the voting age from 21 to 18) without any other word being changed. It can be done. This should be done before all the possible negative consequences become overwhelming. We have to quit rewarding people for cheating the system.

FAMILY

To show how absurdly anti-marriage we have become in our society, let me give an example. Mr. Matt Daniels is executive director of the Alliance for Marriage (AFM). He has formed a coalition of many backgrounds from across the nation to support his Federal Marriage Amendment to the Constitution of the United States. This Amendment states: "Marriage in the United States shall consist only of the union of a man and a woman. Neither this Constitution or the Constitution of any state, nor state or federal law, shall be construed to require that marital status or the legal incidents thereof be conferred upon unmarried couples or groups."

To most Americans, having to make an amendment to the US Constitution just to say marriage is between a man and a woman seems as absurd as doing the same to tell people not to leave a newborn baby out in the snow for a week. And yet, the anti-family types, especially the homosexual lobby, have made it a priority to put the last nail in the coffin of traditional marriage. The Center for Arizona Policy newsletter, dated June 13, 2002 said: "According to Gary Bauer, a recent poll of 1,500 self-identified homosexuals found that the number one goal of homosexuals is the legal recognition of same sex marriage."

Once you have broken the one-man-one-woman mold of marriage, what is next? Why not one-man-three-women? How about one man and his sheep? One man and a ten-year-old boy? A woman and two little girls? This all sounds ridiculous but once again, we are brought back to opening the floodgates. You cannot open a floodgate just a little bit.

THE MARRIAGE FRONT

One of the greatest successes of the liberal establishment on its long war on marriage is its use of financial discrimination against it.

This is a four-pronged attack: (1) The marriage penalty on income tax. (2) The Social Security/pension plans marriage penalty. (3) The Welfare discouragement of marriage tactic. (4) Domestic Partner Benefits used to eliminate the last financial advantage to marriage.

(1) The marriage penalty is the simplest. If you and your fiancee earn $30,000 apiece, the two of you together, as of this filing season, will pay a total of $8,906 in federal income taxes using the short form. If you had gotten married last year and

filed "married, filing jointly," using the short form, you would have paid $10,003 in federal income taxes. By lumping the money together, you went to a higher tax bracket and have to pay an additional $1,097 in taxes every year from now on.

(A) For example: Several years ago I was sent by my company to a training facility for a three-week class. I became friends with a fellow student I will call "Jerry." We studied together and during breaks talked about our lives and learned about each other. He kept on mentioning his "girlfriend." They moved in together fifteen years ago. They had two children together. In twelve more years they would retire, get their pensions and then they were going to get married.

After piecing together this and other information, the last week of class, when we were studying together one night, I had to ask him. I said: "Jerry, you talk about your girlfriend the way I talk about my wife. Why are you waiting until you retire to marry her?"

He stated that when they first decided they wanted to spend the rest of their lives together, they had intended to get married right away. But then they figured it out and because of the marriage tax penalty, it would cost them over $40,000 in extra taxes spread over their working lifetimes. At the time, that was enough money to buy two brand new Corvettes and pay cash for them; or buy a brand new 1200 square-foot house and pay 60 percent down on it (in most parts of the country.) When they retire, their income will be low enough that it won't make that much difference.

(2) The Social Security penalty takes the same form as the Marriage Penalty above. The pension plan penalty affects mostly widows and widowers. Suppose you and your intended both get (reduced) pensions and health benefits from your deceased spouse. In many pension programs if you remarry, you will lose that pension and those health benefits.

(3) Welfare used to be such that if a woman was on welfare, if she got married, she lost her benefits. This was a battle that was defined in Newt Gingrich's Contract with America. Under the welfare reform that resulted, more people are getting back to

work, fewer people are unable to find a job for three generations, and the welfare punishments for getting married were reduced. This is a front on which America is now in the process of winning.

(4) Domestic partner benefits for the unmarried. This is a two-edged sword. On the one hand, it advances the homosexual agenda. But, to get it to look good to a wider section of the populace, the benefits are worded such that it extends the benefits to unmarried heterosexuals who just live together, with no formal or legal commitments. This adds insult to injury. Besides avoiding all the punishment listed above for getting married, if domestic benefits are available to you, you can have many of the financial benefits of marriage and still "not get hooked."

HISTORY REVISIONISM

History revisionism has gone from annoying to maddening to insufferable. When I was studying the history of the Middle East back around 1970 I discovered that if you asked a bunch of historians what the greatest historical tragedy was, the answer you would get would differ depending on each historian's specialty. But if you asked what are the top five greatest historical tragedies it is probable that one item would be on every list. This would be the destruction of the famed Library at Alexandria. These citizens had gone to great lengths (sometimes immoral lengths) to get the original copies, or at least the oldest copies of as many of the greatest writings in the world as they could. My history class around 1970 taught that most of the library and the priceless treasures it contained were destroyed by the Muslims as infidel writings. Also there was a small "branch" or annex in today's terms that was destroyed by a fanatical Christian sect. Just recently, I saw a history special on PBS that said that Christians destroyed the Library at Alexandria, with no mention of anything being touched by Muslims! How history has changed!

This was a few years ago when history revisionism was annoying. The reason it is insufferable now is that they are revising history practically as it happens.

Two examples of this instant history revisionism are: (1) after 1994, the new Republican majority in Congress fought tooth and nail to get welfare reform passed. But Clinton hated this attempt to dismantle Johnson's Great Society (which had been a total disaster.) Clinton vetoed the legislation until a bipartisan coalition got enough votes to pass it over his veto, so he signed it; everybody knew this. Yet, after a couple of years, it became obvious that welfare reform was a screaming success. Once this was firmly established, the media gave Clinton the credit for welfare reform!

(2) Bob Dole ran against Clinton for the presidency in 1996. Clinton moved toward the center and started harvesting more votes than he could get from his base of homosexuals, socialists and others on the extreme left (maybe 6 percent or so of the population.) Dole saw this and decided to do the same, move to the center. After all, what would their base do, vote for the other guy? HA HA. Unfortunately for Dole, his base of conservatives, Christians and others was probably four or five times the size of Clinton's base. Though they were both right, their bases did not vote for the other guy, both their bases stayed home and didn't vote at all (figuratively speaking). Clinton lost his 6 percent base and Dole lost his 25 percent base. This caused Clinton to win by a smaller margin than Dole's base could have compensated for. Just four years later, the media told Bush not to make the mistake Dole made, and the reason why he lost the election: He moved from the center to pander to the right wing extremists of the Republican Party. Just the opposite of what really happened four years earlier! (Remembering that in liberal media speak, right wing extremists means conservatives, Christians and anybody who is not 100 percent in favor of the entire homosexual agenda.)

A THEORY GAINING CREDIBILITY

A phrase that has been gaining in popularity over the past twenty years is that "there is no difference between the Republicans and Democrats. They are secretly, behind closed doors on the same side." This belief has led to an increasing number of people who classify themselves as Independents.

Most of the time I see a great deal of difference between the Republican party, mostly pro-life, mostly pro-freedom of religion, mostly pro-second amendment rights, and the Democratic party, mostly pro-abortion, mostly anti-Christian, mostly for gun control. But once in a while, I too am made to wonder. For instance:

When the legislature voted to give the sitting president, who happened to be George W. Bush, the line item veto, the Supreme Court immediately "vetoed" the bill as unconstitutional. Maybe it is and maybe it isn't, but it is obviously controversial to the average citizen. Yet, when the McCain/Fiengold "Campaign Finance Reform Bill" passed, an obviously unconstitutional law, the courts did nothing, but waited for a long involved court case to run through the system before they acted. (This bill is colloquially known as the Media Empowerment Act and the Incumbent Assurance Act. It, for all intents and purposes, revokes the First Amendment to the Constitution, the Freedom of Speech clause.) The courts eventually upheld this unconstitutional law.

The fact that both Republicans and Democrats voted for this unscrupulous bill, the fact that Bush, a supposedly conservative president, under the guise of trying to get along, signed it, adds a great deal of credence to those who believe that there is no longer a difference between the major parties. I'm not fully convinced, but I am starting to wonder. The deals being made in smoke-filled back rooms on Capitol Hill seem to be making another front against honesty and straight-dealing. (All right, they probably are no longer allowed to smoke in public buildings, but it's still a neat metaphor.)

Another specific item that tends to add credence to the "no difference" or "they're all on the same side" theory is the lack of caring what the opposition does to one's own supporting base.

During the Clinton years the Internal Revenue Service was "encouraged" to investigate conservative groups (such as the Heritage Foundation) for tax improprieties with absolutely no evidence for such improprieties whatsoever. These "investigations" went on for years and cost the non-liberal organizations hundreds of thousands of dollars to comply with the IRS. (At the end of the Clinton era, these "investigations" ended. No improprieties had been discovered.) Yet, almost no left-wing groups were investigated during this time. Was this a coincidence? Possibly. But what makes one suspicious is that no supposedly conservative politician or Republican has ever asked for an investigation into this blatant discrimination toward groups whose supporters tend to support the reportedly more conservative party. It is almost like someone is attacking a person you say you love, but you do nothing to help your beloved.

LIBERALISM

If you look at all the attacks on America from within and think of them as parts of a body, they would look like a fist hitting you as one front, a foot kicking you at another, and maybe a skull being used as a head-butt. But the central nervous system of all this seems to be liberalism.

Admittedly, almost nobody will confess to being a liberal anymore. As radicals morphed into liberals, now liberals are trying to morph into "centrists" or "moderates" or even "progressives." I hope nobody buys it.

One should ask, "Why do liberals want to destroy America?" I do not think they started out with that in mind as a goal. I believe most liberals started out as idealists who thought they had a better way. What has ironically happened is that they have become the very things they started out rebelling against. This has happened for the very same reason that the old establishment became corrupt. Absolute power always corrupts those who attain it. The closer you get to it, the more corrupt you become. That is why our founding fathers designed a system that made "certain" that no one body of thought would take over and predominate. Yet, they made certain that eventually all bodies of thought could participate. The will of the mass of the people would temper the extremes and make sure no one person or one group would become dictatorial. They did not count on the power of mass propaganda or on the loss of our country's Christian foundation.

Liberalism may have finally, after over two hundred years of our existence, found a way around all those safeguards. They seem to have realized that one of the things that kept the people stable was the Christian foundation. An anti-Christian propaganda campaign that has not let up for forty years has done much to destroy that foundation. Capitalism empowers ordinary people; there has been a legislative agenda to erode capitalism and replace it with class warfare and socialism. The American culture based in these and other things that do not lend themselves to the tyranny of a single group is being slowly replaced by multiculturalism. Liberalism is willing, now, to bring us to the edge of chaos, so that they can be the heroes and bring order through tyranny.

The hypocrisy of liberals is so built in that it is sometimes compulsive. I was watching one of the last network "Donohue" shows, since it was about to go off the air. This particular one was about creation versus evolution. The three-person, "unbiased" panel of experts all made at least part of their livings off propounding of evolution. During the first quarter of the show, Phil said that these creationists say there are a lot of closet creationists who are scientists, but they are SO PARANOID that they do not let this fact be known for fear of discrimination. About one half hour later Phil says: You know what we should do? We should have, on those tests that all high school seniors take, a question on whether the students believe in evolution or not. And if they don't believe in evolution, they should not be allowed to go on to any institutions of higher education. Thus, Phil Donohue proposed the very type of discrimination against "them" that they would have to be paranoid to believe that anyone would propose, according to him. His hypocrisy is so ingrained as a liberal, he no longer notices it.

One of the biggest mind tricks pulled on us is accusing those who oppose them of being what they themselves are and of doing what they themselves do. For example, they accuse others of censorship. Yet they can name the few conservatives that the major media has allowed to have work. Nobody can name the thousands of liberals in the major media.

Liberals claim the right is not fair and does not follow the law. Yet, when Gore lost the Florida electoral votes by Florida law, the all-Democrat Florida Supreme Court chose to ignore the law and decided to keep the recounts going after the legal deadline, hoping to find a way to make Gore the winner. And then liberals whined about the law (after the Supreme Court of the US had to step in and make the justices obey the law). Yet after all was said and done, since they knew there was nothing wrong with the law and next time it could just as easily work in their favor, nobody introduced any legislation to change it.

It is interesting to watch their tactics evolve. As I mention elsewhere they went from twisting the law, such as finding a right to abortion in the Constitution, to just ignoring the law, such as the New Jersey Supreme Court deciding to allow a replacement for a Democratic senatorial candidate when the law said it was too late to do so. Now maintaining and ever increasing their own power is all that matters. Since Americans are the freest people on Earth, and no despotic force can rule a free people, our freedom must be destroyed for them to gain any more power. One of the goals every leftist organization (People for the American Way, ACLU, all homosexual organizations, Americans United for the Separation of Church & State, et al) has in common is the total revocation of the Bill of Rights. They want to do away with your individual rights and have special rights for leftists that trump everyone else's rights.

So the next time you think about voting for a liberal politician because he: (1) is just trying to help me with more welfare benefits; (2) is just trying to protect me with gun control legislation. (3) is just protecting a minority by sponsoring gay rights legislation. (4) is just protecting us from those religious nuts by shutting down public acknowledgment of Christianity. (5) is just being fair to unmarried couples by punishing married couples with more taxes, less pension benefits, etc. Please realize that what they are really doing is destroying everything that made this country great in order to establish a power base from which you, the people, will no longer be able to remove them.

Leftists believe that they are doing humanity a favor by trying to rid society of the three "Cs": Christianity, Capitalism and Conservatism. By getting rid of traditional morality, this will make everyone so much freer. What they do not seem to realize is that what they are attempting to do is rip the foundation out from under the USA. And just like would happen with a house if you ripped out the foundation, the rest collapses. Even if this collapse is their intended purpose, they must presume that they will emerge from the rubble as the leader, and this is not necessarily the way it will be.

ISN'T COMPROMISE ALWAYS RIGHT?

One thing that I wish conservatives would remember is that when you compromise with liberals, they will use your compromise against you.

For instance: When George H. W. Bush (41) compromised with the liberals in Congress by raising taxes, they then used it very effectively against him by constantly bringing up that he raised taxes after his "read my lips, no new taxes" statement in ads during his bid for reelection. He quite literally lost his second term in office because he did what they wanted, instead of what he felt was right.

Twelve years later, George W. Bush (43) got into office with that same "can't wait to start compromising" attitude and sure enough, he starts giving in on education and other things, the budget goes up and they blame him for the return to deficits; not that he doesn't deserve some of the blame, but without his accusers' help, we would still have surpluses.

His biggest compromise was signing the "media empowerment and incumbent protection" act into law. I mean "Bi-partisan Campaign Finance Reform Bill." People may eventually realize how much freedom that bill takes away from them, and, later, how it opened the floodgates to taking many more freedoms away. But if they do, I guarantee that the liberals will blame George W. and the people will hold it against him but not every senator and congressman who voted for it, the way they should. But then again, under this law, most of the people who would remind you of who voted for it are not allowed to inform you of that, at least not for the sixty days before the election. (AKA McCain/Fiengold+Shays/Mehan.).

GOALS OF A MOVEMENT

Liberalism has become synonymous with corruption. In their heart of hearts, they do not understand what is wrong with lying, cheating, redefining terms, falsely accusing others of impropriety, etc.; as a means to a noble end. That end being them in charge of everything and everyone under the complete control of the government.

Then abortion clinics will be as common and as welcome as theaters; all honest Americans will be disarmed; nobody will be allowed to say anything politically incorrect or they will be fined into poverty and spend time in federal prison. Homosexuality will be taught to grade school children and as many turned to that lifestyle as possible prior to puberty, when they are the most vulnerable. Christianity, with all its standards and morality and influences on the American culture will have been replaced by liberalism's standards and morality, and history will be totally rewritten to ignore the church's previous existence. Capitalism will be out, socialism in. Somehow, to them, this will be the ideal society, when everyone is equally poor, equally powerless, and equally miserable—everyone except them, the leaders of the liberal movement. Notice that the working class liberals will probably be just as poor as the rest of us, but they will at least be allowed to speak their minds since they agree with the powers that be.

Knowing how hysterically liberals scream when anyone suggests they are wrong; they will interpret the above few paragraphs as implying that everyone should go out and kill liberals; I must, therefore make the following clear: liberals deserve freedom of speech and expression as well as everyone else. However, it is the responsibility of the vast majority of our citizens—YOU AND I— to vote our intellectually realized common sense and keep them out of power. We must keep ourselves informed enough not to fall for their irrational, illogical and freedom destroying rhetoric.

TRICKS OF THE TRADE

Diversity has become another push-button word to make you think liberalism is a gathering place for all the different types of people. This could not be further from the truth.

Referring to the *New York Times* and its attempts to keep Jayson Blair as a reporter after it knew he made up "news" stories, probably to maintain its diversity (he is black), Gene Edward Veith said it better than I can: "...diversity has to do with skin color, rather than diversity of ideas. People are supposed to look different but think alike.... In addition to the goal of having a newsroom 'that looks like America,' editors should aim at having a newsroom that thinks like America."[176]

One of the most effective litanies of the left during debates is, "Are you questioning my patriotism?" or some variation of this.

It is a great ploy because the conservative debater is always trying to be the nice guy, looking for compromise, not wanting to offend anyone. Almost always, it puts the conservative on the defensive and gets him to back off, and apologetically so.

Yet, look at what the liberal, in his heart of hearts really wants. He wants to erase all knowledge of the Christian foundation of this country. He wants to repeal the First Amendment of the Constitution (freedom of speech, for example, McCain/Feingold; freedom of religion by making it illegal to express your religion in any way in the public arena); revoke the Second Amendment ("the right of the people to keep and bear arms, shall not be infringed." by regulations, fees and laws that infringe on that right); ignore the Fourteenth Amendment (...nor shall any state deprive any person of life, liberty or property, without due process of law"; abortion deprives millions of persons of life without due process—what capital crime have they committed?)

Therefore, what they want to do is replace the United States of America's government and culture with some other form of society and system of laws. Is there any better definition of being unpatriotic? When liberal activist judges make such inane rulings as saying that saying the Pledge of Allegiance in public schools is unconstitutional because of the phrase "under God," this implies that reading the Constitution in school is also

---

176 Vieth, Gene Edward. "Peddling poppycock" *World Magazine* 31 May 2003: 13.

unconstitutional because of the phrase "the Year of Our Lord"— a direct reference to Jesus—in article seven. Also the reading of the Declaration of Independence would be unconstitutional because of the phrases, "nature's God" and "endowed by their Creator."

Our founding fathers thanked God, implored God and referred to God throughout the process of founding this country. Liberalism would remove all references to God from the public arena and I believe that George Washington, Abraham Lincoln, Benjamin Franklin, John Adams, and many other great Americans would call that unpatriotic.

BRAINWASHING CAN BACKFIRE

After the 2002 midterm elections, the Democratic congressmen voted to have Nancy Pelosi as the Minority Leader in the House of Representatives. This election had been only the second in 140 years where the president's party (Republican at this time) gained seats in an off-year election. It seemed pretty obvious to us conservatives that the reason the Republican Party gained seats and the Democrats lost was because the GOP had stood for traditional family and patriotic values while the Democratic leadership had stuck to its leftist guns. Yet Pelosi's election to a powerful leadership position showed that the Democratic leadership not only didn't realize the country's right of center leanings, but it felt that a move to the left was what it needed to pick up more votes next election!

At first this totally confused me. How could they miss the obvious? Finally I came up with a hypothesis: (A) the establishment for the last forty years has been a liberal establishment. (B) The major media, as part of this establishment, has been brainwashing the general public with a constant flow of leftward biased brainwashing. (C) Ironically, the Democratic leaders themselves have been brainwashed by their own propaganda mechanisms and actually believe that all Americans are of the far left persuasion. (D) Therefore, any failure to gain more power must mean that they did not go far enough to the left! If their self-delusion continues, this could be very good for

America, especially if the citizens continue to get better informed on why conservatism is better for us than liberalism. Then they would keep moving to the left as the voters keep voting more and more leftists out of office.

THE LIBRARY FRONT

This front seems an unlikely war participant. It's kind of like Switzerland declaring war on Canada.

Somehow the liberal establishment has come to include the American Library Association (ALA). In spite of huge popular protests against it, the ALA's position has been that, if they had their way, every computer in every library in the nation would have unlimited access to pornography and in turn that pornography would be available to children of all ages. It would also be available to the pedophiles who prey on those kids. Keep in mind that as part of the liberal establishment, these are the same types of people who have been in a screaming uproar about the words "under God" being in the Pledge of Allegiance. Blocking pornography to kids is censorship, but erasing all references in every historically viable document that mentions God is somehow not. Does that sound reasonable and fair to you?

One of the most important things you must remember about liberals is that "fair" is defined as "always getting everything our way all the time." "Unfair" is anything else.

To give specific examples of the above: The Supreme Court overturned the Communications Decency Act in 1996. The Child Online Protection Act was struck down in 1998. In 2002 the Children's Internet Protection Act of 2000 was overruled by three federal judges.[177] These three rulings, plus others by other liberal judges, have the effect of upholding the rights of pornographers and pedophiles to practice their perversions by allowing them to peddle their wares to our children online. The ALA is in complete agreement with the pornographers. Their official policy is that pornography should be available, even to computers used almost exclusively by children.

---

177 Munsil, Len. The Center for Arizona Policy Newsletter 31 May 2002.

The liberal establishment screams that the courts are stocked with conservative judges those rare times that the judge follows the dictates of the law, instead of ignoring the law and/or standards of decency to move forward the liberal agenda. The American people need to know what sometimes escapes them: He who yells the loudest is not always in the right. Allowing sexual predators access to our children is not an exercise in freedom of speech. But as long as you keep electing liberal politicians, they will appoint and approve judges who say that it is.

HISTORY VERSUS REVISIONIST HISTORY

"On August 1, 2001, Alabama Supreme Court Chief Justice Roy Moore authorized the placement of a 5200 pound granite monument in the rotunda of the Alabama State Judicial Building located in Montgomery, Alabama.

"The monument depicts the moral foundation of law in America, and bears the text of the Ten Commandments.... The monument also bears quotes from: the Declaration of Independence ('Laws of Nature and of Nature's God'); our National Motto ('In God We Trust'); the Pledge of Allegiance ('One nation, under God, indivisible, with liberty and justice for all'); and the Judiciary Act of 1789 ('So Help Me God')."[178]

Though it is obvious from the quotes on the monument itself that our forefathers had no intention of restricting public expression of our dependence on God by government officials doing the business of governing, the ACLU, Americans United for Separation of Church and State and the Southern Poverty Law Center, within sixty days filed a suit to have this monument removed because it offended them. What if the ACLU and friends offend me? Should they be removed from public participation as well?

It is time that we did something to stop these screaming, temper-tantrum, childish people from demanding that all the rest of us have to do everything their way all the time. Especially

---

178 Melchior, D. Stephen (2011 Central Ave, Cheyenne, Wy 82001) From a letter
   dated 6 April 2002.

if the precedents for the first two hundred years of our history show them to be totally wrong. True, many of these leftist organizations have multimillionaires who finance them, so they do not need your money; and in our free society, you cannot limit their freedom of speech. But once again, you can stop electing the liberal politicians who will appoint and approve judges who will not only listen to their nonsense, but will legislate from the bench to make their dreams of an atheist/anti-God regime come true.

One of the great subtleties of this entire movement to rid our country of any reference to God outside of church or home is its ultimate goal (of many goals): If we remove God from our society, then there is no higher authority than the government. It is then answerable to nobody. Trust me, by the time they achieve this, the government will no longer be answerable to the people either. The Declaration of Independence states that our inalienable rights are from our Creator. If they are not from God, then the state gives them to you and the state can take them away.

These people believe with all their hearts that the average American is far too stupid to know how to run their own lives. You and I need them to tell us how to live. Taking over the judiciary, then having the judiciary take power from both the legislative and executive branches of government, has been the most successful way to achieve all the goals of the left. Without a reversal of what has been going on for the last forty or more years in this realm, soon every last one of your rights will be given to you or taken away from you at the whim of a liberal establishment.

And for those who think this is a good thing, think about this: What if you give all the power to the government and then it changes and becomes, say, a red-neck establishment? Or some other establishment that is vile to you? Individual freedoms given away are not easily recaptured.

A WAR OF WORDS

This little section of one chapter is the most important part of this book in relation to your being able to resist being brainwashed by the propaganda of the liberal establishment.

In the 1960s there was a group of people with specific ideas that were called "radicals." In the 1980s and 1990s the same people with the same ideas morphed into "liberals." In the new century, the same people with the same ideas are being called "moderates," "middle of the road," and "progressive." Just as there were no radicals to be found in the 1990s, soon there will be no "liberals" left.

The point being that you have to be very observant about the language being used, as it is used to control you. You frequently hear the term "far right extremist." Have you noticed that you very rarely hear the term "far left extremist" from the mainstream media? Of course, they are so far to the left, they don't see anyone to the left of themselves, so figure there is no left extreme since they are middle of the road, in their minds.

To give a specific example: When Senator John Kerry said that he would be willing to filibuster George W. Bush's Supreme Court nominees he continued: "...Any person who thinks it's his or her job to push an extreme political agenda rather than to interpret the law should not be a Supreme Court justice."[179] You have a gut negative reaction to those extremist judges he is referring to. But he is defining as extreme those that would uphold the Constitution as written. He defines judges that "interpret the law" as the type of judges that found the rights to abortion and sodomy specifically outlined in the Constitution of the United States of America. I think Washington, Jefferson and Madison would think those judges are insane!

What would be laughable in the misuse of language to control people is when they use the phrase "we don't have" an outlet like Rush Limbaugh to get our message out. They pretend they are little David to the Goliath EIB network. They portray themselves as a hobbit battling a giant when, if you think about it, the reverse is true.

They have made it so you have to take the energy to think through what they are trying to make you feel by the words they use. But if you don't do this, they will control you. That is why it is so important to think things through.

---

179 Author unlisted. From "E-legal eagles" *World magazine* 5/12 July 2003: 66.

Around the year 2000 was when I first noted Tom Daschle portraying himself as little David versus Goliath right-wing conspiratorial forces. But if you thought it through, you had to laugh at this concept. He was the majority leader of the Senate of the United States of America; other than heads of state (presidents, prime ministers and kings) that alone would make him one of the few hundred most powerful people in the world. Add to it that at that time the liberal establishment had picked him to be their presidential candidate for either 2004 or 2008. He had almost unstoppable power. (Unfortunately for Tom, he got "drunk" with power and started spouting off such extreme partisanship and turned off so many voters, the media had to dump him as a presidential hopeful.) To portray himself as the little guy, the underdog, was laughable. But liberals must have thought it worked, because others have used this ploy since.

If the media quits using the word "radical" and you think there are no more radicals, they've got you. If they put the label "right wing extremist" on everyone who disagrees with the liberal agenda and you have a negative gut reaction to that person or group, they are controlling you with their use of words. This is the largest and most effective use of propaganda. You must consciously weigh how words are being used to manipulate you. I feel almost foolish having to say that, but I must because this has been working so well for the liberal establishment for so long. Normal, decent, honorable, everyday Americans keep electing some people to high office whose morals and belief systems are so bad that those same Americans would not even associate with them if they knew them personally. Sometimes this happens solely because the media has told them that the person's opponent is a "right wing extremist."

The propaganda, the use of words to control us, has become so good (in an evil sort of way) that all of us are affected by it. It is up to you to be aware enough to minimize its effect. Even I find myself being affected and influenced by it, and I think most people would not consider me a moderate or liberal.

The other big component of propaganda is repetition. A statement may be an obvious lie the first time it is said. But it magically can seem to become truth if it is repeated enough times.

During his time in a position of power, the media used many variations of language to inform you that Newt Gingrich was evil. Have you ever read his book, *To Renew America*? You cannot read the book without some doubt creeping into your mind about this being a sinister man. Dan Quayle was called stupid (in many ways, with many different words), but have you read his book, *Standing Firm*? This could not have been written by a fool. Rush Limbaugh repeatedly is called things like "the most dangerous man in America" and one, through repetition, we are led to believe who would take an ax to liberals if he gets too close to them. He is a right-wing extremist, a red neck, someone who would enslave us if he could. Read his book *The Way Things Ought To Be* and find yourself totally perplexed when you think of what you've been told to think about him by the mainstream media.

I might even say that if you hear something time and time again in the media, especially if it is negative and about a single person or group, start doubting what they are saying, or at least analyze it thoroughly. Go find out what the people they are denigrating really believe. Even some liberal writers have left their ivory towers and gone to some meeting of "right-wing extremist" groups (like some Bible-believing church convention) and been shocked that they were not hate-filled, screaming bigots.

Another thing is to look for absurdities in logic. Like when the media demonized Christians who are elected representatives to a convention actually trying to get candidates elected that agree with their agenda! As opposed to those delegates that vote for candidates who represent the opposite of their point of view? (This idea paraphrased from Ann Coulter's book *Slander*.)

It seems so unfair that we have to use so much energy thinking about everything we hear from the powers that be, but many of our forefathers fought and died to give us the rights that make us free, and expending mental energy to preserve those rights is a small price to pay. Once you lose those freedoms, the price you pay to get them back goes way up!

COMPLACENCY

Winning on a front is particularly difficult when you have already lost a lot of ground.

As this new millennium is starting to unfold, people are more and more willing to relinquish their rights and freedoms in America. It has already happened to a staggering degree.

When Shays-Meehan (McCain/Fiengold in the Senate) became law, it did little in the way of campaign finance reform, which was what the authors called it, but it did much to empower the liberal media and make incumbents running for reelection much more likely to be successful. Further, on the collective level, it almost entirely repealed the second right of the First Amendment, freedom of speech. They imply, "Well, you can still go door to door and tell your neighbors how your congressman voted." It is just that you cannot give money to, say, Christian Coalition, or many other organizations, and have them send out millions of voter guides to tell a great number of people how all the politicians voted on issues sixty days before a general election. Do I need to point out that the last sixty days is the only time most people get interested in the election? Where were the recall elections when the majority of your representatives voted away this part of your freedom of speech?

Another example of us allowing our representatives in all levels of government to relieve us of our rights is in the area of the right to bear arms.

There are an estimated twenty thousand regulations, at all the various levels of government that restrict your right to bear and keep arms. All but a few of them (regarding convicted felons, supervision of minors, etc.) are unconstitutional. Your right to bear arms has been severely infringed. But the vast majority of the American people seem lulled into some sort of complacent trance with regard to the taking away of their freedoms.

For the last forty years it has been more and more this way: If you, as a student in a public school, or a working class civil servant, expressed your freedom of speech by saying, writing, or communicating your strong opinions in favor of Christianity, pro-life, gratitude to God for His blessings, the need for a return to morality, then you would risk a lawsuit by the ACLU, suspension from work or school, or some establishment authority telling you that your rights have been suspended in these areas.

But if an equally vociferous person communicated in favor of atheism, pro-abortion, pornography, gay pride, anti-Americanism, or any other leftist cause, they still have their freedom of speech. When freedoms are retained only for one side, they are no freedoms at all. They are a type of dictatorship disguised as freedoms.

This complacency is allowing the erosion of our freedoms, not only without protest, but without notice by the very people who are losing their freedoms. I cannot help but suspect that this is the result of some kind of brainwashing brought about by the constant mantras of the liberal establishment through the propaganda ministry—I mean the media. Just a wild guess and I am by far not the first to have mentioned it. If this is a new concept to you, you definitely need to search out other sources of information, a few of which are listed in Appendix One at the back of this book.

THE FISCAL FRONT

Everybody seems to complain about rampant overspending by the government. But everything just keeps on going on the same to the constant irritation and confusion of the average person.

What we do not seem to understand is that we have institutionalized overspending such that the people in charge cannot change if they want to. And, unfortunately, governments can spend themselves into ruin just as individuals can.

For instance, if your department has a budget of $10 million, you are forced to spend it, or have your budget cut. This is one of those "brilliant" ideas that was intended to prevent government waste and has had exactly the opposite effect. The theory was, if they allocated you $10 million, and you only spent $9 million, they would cut your budget and save $1 million. Human nature being what it is, nobody wants their budget cut and they can always find ways to spend whatever they have.

To give an analogy, suppose a person earns $50,000/year. What is he going to spend? $50,000. Suppose he is industrious and starts earning $100,000/year. How much is he going to spend? $100,000. "Wait a minute," you say, "He might save $20,000 of the $100,000." But, suppose there were a weird rule that if he saved $20,000, the next year he would only get $80,000. Once again, he would spend $100,000. That's really how governments work. This rule exists for them.

I would propose changing this by telling everybody that their budget will not be cut unless the scope of their operation or their manpower is reduced. Also, their next year's budget increase would be tied to inflation or the CPI or some other reasonable measure. Then, if they come in under budget, 50 percent of the money they saved will be put into a lock box fund for their department to be accumulated toward capital or other needs in the future; 49 percent would go back into the general fund, or a general rainy-day fund. An example might be, five years down the road, remodeling, or building a new building. So, if they save $1 million/year, in five years, they will have 2.5 million in the savings account for a special project. The present system forces people to be dishonest and wasteful with no reasonable alternative. I remember my father, when he worked for LA County, saying that at the end of one fiscal year, the people who did the budget were going out and buying enough typewriters and pens and pencils, etc., to last for the next ten years because they "*had* to spend the money." Can you imagine the waste of having two hundred typewriters in a storeroom, five years old, but in mint condition since they had never been used, because PCs and word processing took over?

As an incentive to save money, 1 percent of the money saved by a department could be put in a random drawing of all the employees in that department each year; this would include everyone from the custodian to the department head. Therefore, if your unit had one hundred employees and you were $1 million under budget that year, some lucky employee picked at random would get a $10,000 bonus! That's motivation.

EVERY ACCUSATION A MIRROR

One thing that I have learned about the left is that most of the time they accuse the right of some terrible trait or action, they themselves are the ones actually guilty of having that evil trait or practicing that horrible action.

Just to show that this is an international characteristic, listen to this: "The tyrant thinks that he is capable of enslaving people and besieging their freedom, their decisions, and their legitimate choices." Saddam Hussein, referring to President George W. Bush. This was after Saddam had been in power in Iraq for almost thirty years and through torture, genocide and whim had killed an *average* of thirty thousand of his own citizens every year while in power.

Some other writer may expand on this list and write his own book just on this topic. But from these examples I hope you can see that the war of values, the war to keep Americans free and America wealthy and strong, is a war that needs you and me as soldiers. If the vast majority of Americans remain uninvolved, just unthinkingly following whatever the liberal establishment tells them, doesn't take any action, we will lose our freedom, chances for wealth, and Creator- endowed rights to life, liberty and the pursuit of happiness.

There is a symptom that will show if we are winning or losing the war. If McCain/Feingold causes people to spend jail time or get fined for publishing things about incumbents sixty days before a general election; if because of the *Lawrence v. Texas* supreme court decision, this and other cases lead to people being arrested or fined for speaking in a way that offends some gay person, then you are being fined or arrested for expressing non-establishment thoughts. This only happens in countries where the people are no longer a free people. It may be a symptom that the Christian foundation and traditional American culture are gone since that foundation and culture are what made us a free nation; but in any event, it will mean we are no longer a free people.

Chapter 13

A Winnable War

Before you get too upset about how the foun-dation and the main supports of the United States of America are getting sabotaged, realize that we have been here before. The judicial front seems horrible and irreversible, but an old Supreme Court in the Dred Scott decision decided that people could be nothing more than property. That was reversed as freedom grew over time. We overcame the Axis powers after a crippling blow to Pearl Harbor. Bad economic policies laced with circumstance, chance and the panic brought on the Great Depression. But we came out of it and changed policies such that it has never happened here again.

The following article may be illuminating. Although it is about a Canadian, it could just as well be set in the US.

POOR CLERGYMAN
DOESN'T KNOW HE'S AFFLICTED

"An interesting case study came to light recently of a man who has been brain-washed and doesn't know it.

"It did not appear in one of the professional psychiatric journals, however, but as a column in a daily newspaper, and the victim himself, which is to say the writer of the column, was plainly unaware how tragically his column discloses his condition.

"…it's pertinent that he is an Anglican clergyman and sometime academic.

"…He was writing on the gay marriage issue, and he wanted the world to know that, even though he is 'a church-going, Bible-reading, creed-affirming Christian,' he is whole-heartedly in favour of gay marriage.

"All through his life this man has watched the advance of the 'common good,' he writes.

"Things like the decriminalization of contraception back in the '20s, the legalization of Sunday sports in the '40s, the easing of the divorce laws in the '60s, the legalization of abortion in the '70s, and now with the new century, the crowning achievement, the legalization of gay marriage.

"'Canadians have learned to live with successive changes in lifestyle, each one feared as the first step on a slippery slope,' he writes. 'Yet we have remained a peaceable kingdom… Laws in a pluralistic society must embrace everyone. This country is a better place to live for all of us when we acknowledge we can be different without fighting about it. Or repressing it.'

"Now the fascinating aspect of all this is that while the man knows that great changes have occurred in our society, he does not realize that equally great changes have also occurred within himself.

"He does not reflect that if anyone had told him during the days of the Sunday sports controversy that one day he would be fervidly approving of abortion on demand, he would have considered the suggestion absurd.

"And if anyone had mentioned to him when he was enthusiastically endorsing abortion on demand that one day he would with equal zeal be approving of sodomy as the sexual basis of a marriage, he would have dismissed the idea as preposterous.

"Similarly, if anyone today suggested that 20 years hence, he would be avidly endorsing pedophilia and polygamy, he would respond with the same shock and horror.

"But he would be there all right, eagerly affirming that 'laws in a pluralistic society must embrace everyone.'

"Not only is this clergyman unaware of the changes within himself, neither does he suspect that these radical revisions in his views didn't just happen. They were caused. Such is his piteous state.

"Caused by whom or what, one asks.

"Caused by the media.

"Caused by the new fashions in academe.

"Caused by the education establishment.

"Caused by the 'spirit of the age.'

"Caused by the ancient human quest to somehow escape the demands of conscience and morality.

"We are 'free,' we proclaim, not realizing we have become more thoroughly enslaved than almost any previous generation.

"We can be manipulated, fashioned, shaped, molded.

"Put the right spin on some new 'freedom,' support it with editorials and columns in the 'authoritative' newspapers, furnish it with the respected academic credentials, let the judges loose on it, and in 30 years you could have a man like this swinging from the trees with a banana in his mouth, all the while gibbering: 'This country is a better place to live for all of us, when we acknowledge we can be different.'

"What, I wonder, is the basis of this thing he calls 'the common good'?

"Where does it come from? What is its authority?

"Is it merely whatever the majority favours?

"If the majority approved of, say, slavery, does that mean slavery must serve the common good?

"Why is it that sodomy was considered criminally evil 40 years ago and is now so sacrosanct that to even criticize it is to risk prosecution?

"Those are big questions.

"The trouble is that long ago this unfortunate man quit asking them."[180]

---

180 Byfield, Ted. "Poor clergyman doesn't know he's afflicted" *Christian Renewal* 12 Jan 2005: 18 & 37.

When the American people realize that something is very wrong, they can rise up to the occasion, make it right and go back to the principles that made this the greatest experiment in freedom the world has ever seen.

That is what this book is about. People have a vague feeling that something is terribly wrong, that the US has lost its way and is about to stumble into a disaster from which it will not recover. This book is meant to inform everyone about what is wrong so that now the American people can make it right. We can avoid the disaster.

The media will tell you that I'm living in the past; Americans cannot be the way I describe anymore. They say this, not because it is impossible, but because they are ordering you not to be that way. They are telling you that you cannot be squeaky clean, moral, honest, and have the courage of politically incorrect convictions. They will brainwash you from having any chance to believe in a biblical God. He does not fit into the society they believe they have created.

But I have faith in you. Liberalism has been a form of backsliding. To those who will not follow its lead they want to bring back bigotry, discrimination and censorship. Those who are unwilling to fall into line will be called names, have a harder time finding a job, and suffer other kinds of persecution—for a time. But when the rest of the Americans realize that their freedoms are being systematically taken away, one by one, then those who would enslave the rest of us will find out that they never stood a chance of winning. Right now, you can still participate and not just change the world, but save the world. You can still vote, you can still write, call or e-mail your congressmen and other representatives, you can still be heard. You can quit being a sexual predator and make the commitments that come with being an honorable man. Women can quit being willing victims and have the self-confidence to stand up for their own purity. We must not only win on the political front, but in the home too. If we win all else and let the family die, we can still lose.

Now that you know what the plan has been, now that you have had a glimpse of what a dreadful future it will be if it continues, now you can make sure it doesn't happen. Contact some of the politically incorrect organizations and find out which politicians are trying to take away your constitutional rights. Who voted to end First Amendment free speech with the Feingold/McCain bill (and Shays/Mehan); who voted to end freedom of the press with the Crush Rush bill; who voted to end the Second Amendment with licensing and registration and other infringements on the right to keep and bear arms? Vote them out of office and keep voting for people who will restore your rights. (Or for the super heroes: Recall election anyone?)

We will win this war without a shot being fired. The American people will not wait until all their rights have been taken away before they get us back on the right track.

The left counts on you being easily brainwashed, stupid, lazy and easily fooled. As long as you do nothing, they will win. I know you better. Now that you know, you will get out there and fight and win. In the long run, they never had a chance.

Chapter 14

Israel and Palestine

W hy on Earth is there a chapter on 'peace in the Middle East' in a book on saving America?" I'm glad you asked.

This is here because the Israel/Palestine problem is a constant thorn in America's side. The conflict is a major excuse (not reason) for terrorism against the US. If we don't solve this problem, true it won't cause America to fall, but in the decades ahead, it will be used to justify hundreds of attacks on our friends as well as dozens of attacks on us. So let's get on with it, quit trying "solutions" that don't work, and solve the problem.

From 1993 to April 2002 there were 149 suicide, or homicide, bombers in Israel, 94 percent of them from the West Bank and Gaza. (Statistics from *Newsweek*, 4/15/02, Pg. 31.)

This is going to come as quite a shock to many politicians worldwide, but Israel and Palestinians, or other Muslim groups, have been at war for almost sixty years now. "Peace in the Middle East" has been the goal of everybody in the world except the Palestinians, their predecessors and their supporters.

When are our leaders going to accept the fact that if it is considered normal for members of a group to regularly tie several pounds of explosives around themselves, walk into a crowd of innocent people and then blow themselves and many of these strangers to pieces, that we are not dealing with normal, rational people? Negotiation and reason will not work.

In the 1990s Israel offered the Palestinians virtually everything they said they wanted: as much land as the Jews could possibly give and still exist, self-rule, real power in Jerusalem, etc. They were turned down. All solutions that leave Jews alive and Israel in existence are unacceptable from their point of view. Any solution that leaves the Jews and the Palestinians living next to each other is like forcing two sworn enemies that have vowed to kill each other to live in the same house. The following is a letter that I sent to President Bush at the beginning of the second Iraq war.

"Dear Sir:

I have an unusual suggestion to consider for accomplishing peace in the Middle East, regarding that facet that revolves around the Israel/Palestine problem.

Since we are temporarily taking over Iraq anyway, why don't we offer a piece of it as the New Palestine? Take an area approximately the size of the entire state of Israel, about 7800 square miles, less than 5% of Iraq's total area. Take it out of the most useless desert region that almost nobody has used for the last 500 years, but guarantee that the USA will hire Palestinians as workers to build canals from the Tigris and Euphrates to supply plenty of water to the region. Further, we will build three or four main cities, factories, etc., for jobs. We will also supply all the fertilizer, gypsum, etc. needed to prepare as much land as needed for crops. We will build modest, but nice housing. [This line should have been: "We will finance and Palestinians will build modest, but nice, housing." Same concept for building cities, etc. Ed. Note]

In exchange for the land, we would rebuild Iraq after the war.

Right now, about 3 million Palestinians live on about 2300 square miles of Israel's 7800 square miles. There are about 6 million Jews in Israel. The Jews have to be getting sick of a constant Jihad being directed against them by the Palestinians and some day either have to expel them or a war will come which may lead to mutual annihilation. It is very obvious that it cannot go on this way.

We could even offer to dismantle, brick by brick if need be, the al-Aqsa Mosque on the Temple Mount in Jerusalem and reassemble it in the center of the new capital city of New Palestine. Or if that would not work, Israel could guarantee Palestinians could come back to Jerusalem to visit the mosque as long as there are no terrorist attacks by Palestinians. [Should have been "offer to pay Muslims to dismantle....Ed. note.]

Yes, I realize this could cost tens of billions of dollars. But if it solved the Israel/Palestine problem, I think most Americans would not mind footing the bill. Or maybe Iraqi oil could pay for it?

Thank you for considering this.

Sincerely, Patrick G. Smith"

Many people say the Palestinians will not accept it (what peace proposal *have* they accepted?) Iraq will hate it. But it has become painfully obvious that there can be no peace with these two living together. This will be hard to do, but it must be done. Let's let their fellow Muslims finally take some of the responsibility for their own brothers.

It is foolish to keep proposing one peace plan after another based on an obviously false premise—that the "Palestinians" and their predecessors want peaceful coexistence. There has never been any objective evidence that would allow us to deduce this premise. Not in fifty-six years! Why allow the fighting to continue? Separate the two main combatants and the fighting will cease, or at least be far more difficult to continue. I know it will not be easy. But it has to be done.

If by the time this book is published, we have lost the opportunity to use our leverage in Iraq and nobody took my suggestion by now, we could offer a good deal to one of the predominantly Muslim, fairly large nations in the neighborhood to do the above plan on their turf. Iraq, Saudi Arabia or Iran has the size to do this. Or, in a worst case scenario, the deal could be made with Libya or Algeria in North Africa, but the water problem would be far more significant. The whole point being that we have to think outside of the box for a real, workable solution.

For those who worry about the explosiveness of transporting the Palestinians, they are right. Think of this analogy. The police in a large American city get a call that correctly informs them that there is a bomb in a certain building downtown. The police confirm this. Removing the bomb is dangerous, it might go off. But would it be better to just leave it there, tell the people to just go back to work and hope it does not blow up? No. The police take the chance, do what they have to and remove the bomb. Usually they get it out somewhere to blow it up harmlessly. Occasionally it blows prematurely. It's a chance you've got to take.

Chapter 15

How You
Can Save America

People are constantly talking about how they cannot understand how "the inmates gained control of the asylum." I hate to say this—nobody needs more to do—but we have to become politically active unless we simply do not care what kind of country we leave to the next generation. Don't worry, the minimum we need to do is easy. Most of us are already doing it.

To give a specific example: In California, the public voted against expanding domestic benefits. This would include extending marriage-type benefits to gays. Shortly thereafter, the California legislature voted to do it anyway. Why would they so obviously go against the will of the people who have the power to vote them out of office? Are they really that ideologically pro-gay—to the point of wanting as much of the homosexual agenda implemented as possible? My answer is: Probably not. But it is all politics. The homosexuals, as a group, are probably the most per capita politically active people in Western civilization. There are around 9 million gays in the US. There are about

280 million heterosexuals (dynamic or potential.) In California there might be 1 million gays and about 30 million heterosexuals. But those state legislators probably received ten letters or phone calls or e-mails for the gay agenda versus one against. Most people hate to get politically active. Most people do not understand that politicians consider that every contact from a constituent represents the feelings of tens, hundreds or even thousands of like-minded voters who don't bother to make the effort. So if 100,000 gays contacted California state legislators about the pro-gay bill, it would have seemed to them that every single person in California was desperate for these bills to pass. The gay lobby can successfully solicit those kinds of numbers from the gay community.

If the moderates and conservatives do not take the time to make contact and support issues or oppose them—send letters, make telephone calls and send e-mails to the politicians—then they will be handing our society over to the forces who are either wittingly or unwittingly destroying the United States of America.

The rest of us must start imitating the left as far as becoming politically active is concerned. We don't have to be as obnoxious; we just have to be as active.

Another example: Who gives money to the American Civil Liberties Union (ACLU)? The ACLU spends literally millions of dollars, every year, to fight for (in favor of) everything listed in this book that will destroy America. (With a small minority of their cases fighting for things I agree with, to their credit.) But the sub-groups that support these things (socialists, gays, anti-Christian bigots, pro "government controlling every aspect of our lives" types) have a much higher percentage of politically active (and financially supportive) people per capita, than moderates or average Americans.

These people have gotten so much un-American legislation passed and gotten so many activist (leftist) judges appointed to legislate from the bench (even though the law forbids them to do so) that the rest of us have no choice but to become politically active or become slaves of the left. Maybe you do not want your daughter to be taught to be a lesbian by the time she is in the sixth grade. Maybe you think every American...even Christians...should have equal freedom of speech rights.

When you just do not feel like getting involved, first remember that just a phone call expressing your point of view on an issue to your representative is all that is needed as a minimum. Second, it might motivate you to remember what Martin Niemoller said:

"In Germany, the Nazis came for the communists and I didn't speak up, because I was not a communist.

"Then they came for the Jews and I didn't speak up because I was not a Jew.

"Then they came for the trade unionists and I didn't speak up because I was not a trade unionist.

"Then they came for the Catholics and I was a Protestant, so I did not speak up.

"Then they came for me. By that time there was no one left to speak up for anyone."

Maybe you do not want your taxes pushed up to 50 percent of your income to support the government that will then control every aspect of your life. These people do want these things, as long as they are at the top of the food chain. And they will be if they remain the most politically active. Becoming active is now the cost of freedom in this country. You can become a soldier in the greatest war that has been fought on this planet. You can be a hero and do something to save the world, whether you are 18 or 88, healthy or crippled, extraordinary or just an ordinary guy or girl. As outlined in this book, if the left gets their way, the USA as we have known it will cease to exist. When our freedom, power and wealth disappear, our stabilizing influence and economic benefits to the rest of the world will stop. Without the US as the hub of the wheel, the rest of the societies will fly apart, out of control. All of the turmoil of the twentieth century will look like the Garden of Eden by comparison to the twenty-first. You can either sit by the sidelines and watch it happen or get involved and quite literally save the world. (See Appendix One for underground organizations that can help inform you on the other side of the issues.)

First of all, register to vote. Do not procrastinate until it is too late, so you can say at the last minute, "I'd like to vote, but I'm not registered." Even those boring midterm elections almost always have something worth voting yes or no on. You do not have to vote on every person or every proposition. It is worth going to vote (or sending in an absentee voting form) even if you vote your conscience on just one person or one issue and leave the rest of the ballot blank.

ENTERTAINMENT

This next one will be the toughest of them all for some of us, so I will start with an example.

Tom Cruise was starring in a Spielberg movie about to be released. I really wanted to see this movie. Then I read an interview with Tom Cruise where he implied that he hated the USA so much that he refuses to raise his kids here and will take them to some other country to educate them. After hearing this, I made the difficult decision that I would just skip that most recent Tom Cruise movie. In fact, I refuse to make this incredibly wealthy man any richer if he hates my country. I will not go to any more Tom Cruise movies, and if you come to the conclusion that Tom hates America and you love America, you should not either. (This is a sacrifice to a one-time movie buff like me. I really hope to find out some day that Tom clarifies that he has come to love America, or that I misinterpreted him. He gets hired to make some very good movies.)

Obviously, my concept here is that we have to start abstaining from watching entertainment that makes people rich who either hate who we are, or want to destroy those things that we believe in. That would include a large number of entertainment personalities.

To be the most effective in reversing our cultural disintegration, I would recommend that you try to determine which TV series are ramming politically correct preaching down your throat every night and stop watching them. If a show pushes, socialism, anti-Christian themes, homosexuality, anti-Americanism, gun control, immorality, the wonderfulness of divorce or adultery, anti-family values, etc., then quit watching the show. To assure they get the message, write the studio or production company, or sponsors, etc., and let them know why you are refusing to watch their show. The best part of that would be to write the sponsors of the show and tell them that if they continue supporting this show, you will quit buying their product. (See Appendix One, Parent's Television Council for a group dedicated to influencing the media for decency.)

For instance, *Will and Grace* is well written, funny and well-acted. If it were unique in the homosexual exposure we receive, I would not have any objections to it, if it played after the kids go to bed. Watching it would be an adult's choice. But when the homosexual lobby is trying and succeeding in taking over the school systems of the different states to indoctrinate the next generation into the homosexual lifestyle, when they are demanding that we turn our children and grandchildren over to them to recruit; when, worldwide, age of consent laws are lowering the age of consent, with the eventual intent of abolishing such laws altogether and making the children vulnerable to sexual predators, and a successful homosexual agenda would take away some of everyone else's rights, then *Will and Grace* and other such exhibits are simply putting a very angelic mask on a very ugly monster.

Foul language and nudity should be avoided, particularly if the kids are around when such shows are aired. Yes, you hear the language at work every day. True, we men cannot help but love looking at beautiful nude women. But it is not hypocritical to fight your natural impulses if you have a good reason. The ever increasing use of vulgar language degrades humankind. If we do not strive to be better than we are, we will drift toward being less than we were. Call it a form of human entropy. I am not saying we all need to try to be perfect; but if we do not try to get to the next higher level, we somehow have a tendency to slip to the next lower level.

As for the nude scenes, they help increase young adults' desires and all the huge factors that make those desires so prevalent (particularly among men) increasing the temptation of premarital and extramarital sex, which you know from my discussion on the sexual revolution, is a bad thing. Admittedly, in a certain type of perfect world, we could all run around naked, weather permitting, and have sex with whomever we choose. But the only people who think this is a perfect world are in serious risk of being institutionalized. Our actions have consequences, so we should not support things that stimulate wrong choices that lead to negative outcomes.

If you want to go the extra mile and become not just active, but an activist, then you could find out which network has the raunchiest programming, boycott that network entirely and write to them that you are doing so and why you are doing this; and don't forget about contacting the sponsors.

If you really want to get involved, this is the next step. Movie studios will continue to produce poorly attended, politically correct propaganda films as long as their other films make enough money to pay for them. You could research which studios are most guilty of this and boycott their other films as well. You should write them and tell them why you are doing this.

POLITICS

Once again, in California the voters rejected domestic benefits for unmarried couples, both hetero and gay. The legislature then ignored them and passed legislation to put it in anyway. When this type of thing happens in your state, you must get out and get the petitions signed to recall those legislators who voted in such a way that they seem to say, "Screw the people, I'll do what certain lobbies pay me to do, and to heck with representing the will of the people." Trust me; you do not want these people in power over you and your children. To make it easier, you might start with just one or two of them, get them removed from office, and see if the others get the message by not opposing the will of the people on the next issue. If they didn't get it and continue doing the opposite of the people's will, remove some more.

REWARDING YOUR ENEMIES

Another thing you can do about all this is when you perceive things, *do something* about the things you take note of.

For instance, after the September 11, 2001 terrorist attack on America, one of the big three network news anchors of that day stated proudly that he refused to wear a flag lapel pin to show solidarity with the American People—he didn't want to be biased against the terrorists—he didn't want to show partiality. Why would any American watch his show after that? It really is OK to love the country that has given (especially given to a rich national news anchor) so unbelievably much to us. It is pure ingratitude not to.

One of the flaws that we Americans have, that we need to work on, is that we keep making multimillionaires of perverts, scam artists, and people who hate America. We pay unbelievable amounts of money to go to concerts, buy CDs and support musicians and singers who, when interviewed, talk about how much they hate us! We are the scum of the Earth to these people, so let's give them another of our week's hard earned wages?·

We seem to say that if someone has been immoral enough, let them write a book about it and we will buy a couple million copies and make them rich. (Think Monica Lewinski.) Is this really what we want to turn the American dream into? We have to quit spending our money to satisfy the more perverse side of our natures. We have to quit rewarding people for lowering our standards (also known as "pushing the envelope"). We have to say that we have had enough before we become so addicted to all that we know is wrong (though we defensively justify it) that we cease to know what is right.

A more subtle example of an ordinary person being able to do something that will have a positive result is this: Remember Columbia University Anthropology Professor Nicholas De Genova, who wished for a million Mogadishus? This anti-American professor has been given the freedom of speech by the blood and the sacrifice of our military personnel's lives to say this. But those American students who would have been his students have the right to, en mass, refuse to sign up for his classes. If nobody signs up for his classes for a few semesters, he may realize that we who love America are sick and tired of spoiled brats who have all the luxuries of living here, but hate the culture that gave them all these opportunities. There is no law that says his free speech must go without consequences, that all the rest of us have to continue supporting those who hate us. For the sake of those paranoids reading this (I know a few of you are out there): I am not saying to hurt the person who hates America. I am not saying break any laws to get back at them. I am saying that you do not have to support them.

If the local ice cream shop owner rants about how much he opposes "X" and you are pro-"X," you have the right to buy your ice cream somewhere else! Especially if "X" represents you, someone or something you love, or the values that make you what you are.

One of the mistakes citizens make is only contacting congressmen and senators when they are negative about something—they tell their representatives they did something wrong. You need to write/fax/e-mail a thank-you when they do something you agree with. Politically active people on the left frequently do this so their representative has no reason to wince every time he sees them coming or reads their names. We on the right or in the center have to wise up.

THE OLIGARCHY

Remember, we have to contact our congressmen and ask them to impeach each judge that usurps power, rules against the Constitution as the founders intended it, or legislates from the bench. If our congressman refuses and we know that thousands have contacted him/her on this, we must find an alternate candidate we can support, and start a recall petition to get rid of the anti-impeachment politician. If we do not stop these usurpers, the Constitution-hating activist judges, they will rule us with an iron fist.

Epilogue

To the left, I would say this: The Christian foundation and traditional American culture have given more freedom to you, and all the other Americans, than any other national system has given to any other people in the world in all of history. Maybe instead of scrapping these things to try something different, you should just be happy and leave things alone.

When the leftist groups in Russia took over during the 1917 revolution, they had a phrase to show their solidarity: "No enemies on the left." When the coalition of leftist parties took over, they agreed to a type of rotation of power starting with a four-year term of Communist rule, since the Communist Party was the biggest. Four years later, when it was time for the next party to take their turn, all the leaders of those other parties had mysteriously disappeared.[181]

By destroying the basic tenets of America, you would have us put right back to where Russia was in 1917. And your particular faction on the left might not be the first to "share" power.

---

181 History of Russia from 1905, History 405, Spring Semester 1980, California State University, Northridge.

Appendix 1

Underground Organizations
(Non-Liberal Establishment Entities)

1) Alliance Defense Fund, 15333 N. Pima Road, Suite 165, Scottsdale, AZ 85260; 480-444-0020; www.alliancedefensefund.org. (A legal group defending freedom of religion, sanctity of life and family values.)

2) American Center for Law & Justice (ACLJ), P.O. Box 64429, Virginia Beach, VA 23467-4429; 757-226-2489 www.aclj.org; Jay Sekulow, Chief Counsel. (A leading legal advocacy group for religious freedoms.)

3) Campaign For Working Families, 2800 Shirlington Road, Suite 605, Arlington, VA 22206; 703-671-8800 www.cwf-pac.com. (A non-partisan political action committee dedicated to electing pro-family, pro-life, pro-free enterprise candidates to state and federal offices.)

4) Capitol Resource Institute; 1414 K St., Suite 200; Sacramento, CA 95814; 916-498-1940; www.capitolresource.org (A California pro-family grassroots advocacy group.)

5) Center for Arizona Policy, 11000 N. Scottsdale Road, Su 120, Scottsdale, AZ 85254; 480-922-3101; 800-FAMILY-1; www.azpolicy.org; info@azpolicy.org. (An Arizona policy group.)

6) Christian Coalition, P.O. Box 37030, Washington, D.C. 20013; 202-479-6900; www.cc.org; (A conservative grassroots political organization. It educates the public and lobbies Congress.)

7) Concerned Women for America; 1015 Fifteenth Street NW, Suite 1100, Washington, D.C. 20005; 1-800-323-2200; www.cwfa.org. (A public policy women's organization.)

8) Eagle Forum; P.O. Box 618, Alton, Il 62002-9903; 618-462-5415; www.eagleforum.org (A grassroots conservative education and lobbying group.)

9) Family Research Council, 601 Pennsylvania Avenue, N.W., Suite 901, Washington, DC 20004, (202) 393-2100; www.frc.org (A group that shapes public debate and formulates public policy defending marriage and the family.)

10) Focus on the Family, P.O. Box 35500, Colorado Springs, CO 80935-3550; 800-a-family (U.S. only); www.family.org. (Christian organization devoted to helping preserve traditional values and the institution of the family.)

11) Free Congress Foundation; 717 Second Street, NE, Washington, D.C. 20002; 202-546-3000; www.freecongress-foundation.org. (Lobbying organization)

12) Heritage Foundation: 214 Massachusetts Ave, NE, Washington, D.C. 20002-4999; or PO Box 97057, Washington, DC 20077-7315; 202-546-4400 www.heritage.org (Edwin J. Feulner). (Conservative think tank that formulates and promotes conservative public policies.)

13) (The) Journal, P.O. Box 207, Manitou Springs, CO 80829; 719-685-9103; Journal@summit.org; www.summit.org (A publication of Summit Ministries.) (A conservative catch-all newsletter.)

14) Liberty Counsel, P.O. Box 540774, Orlando, FL 32854; 407-875-2100; liberty@LC.org. (A civil rights group.)

15) Media Research Center; 325 S. Patrick Street, Alexandria, VA 22314; 703-683-9733; www.MediaResearch.org (also: 1-800-672-1423) (Research and education organization that demonstrates liberal bias in the media.)

16) NRA Institute for Legislative Action, 11250 Waples Mill Road, Fairfax, Virginia 22030; 800-392-8683 www.NRAILA.org (A single-issue advocacy group, not a

conservative organization. Educates public and lobbies for Second Amendment rights.)

17) Parents Television Council, P.O. Box 1855, Merrifield, VA 22116; www.parentstv.org (Also: 707 Wilshire Blvd. #2075, LA, CA 90017; 213 629-9255 or 800-882-6868.) (Lobbies FCC to uphold decency standards in broadcasting. Does research and educates the public on family hostile TV programming.)

18) The Rutherford Institute, P.O. Box 7482, Charlottesville, VA 22906-7482; (804) 978-3888. (A conservative think tank.)

19) Thomas More Law Center, 3475 Plymouth Road, Suite 100, Ann Arbor, MI 48105-2550; 734-827-2001; www.thomasmore.org. (Not-for-profit public interest law firm; it defends religious freedom, family values and sanctity of life. TMLC often fights against the ACLU in court.)

20) Traditional Values Coalition, P.O. Box 5020, Hagerstown, MD 21741-5020; www.traditionalvalues.org (Also: 139 "C" Street, SE, Washington DC 20003; 202-547-8570.) (Has 43,000 member churches; lobbies for traditional values.)

21) WallBuilders, P.O. Box 397, Aledo, TX 76008-0397; 817-441-6044; www.wallbuilders.org (Information and education on what the founding fathers believed. WallBuilders educates citizens and elected representatives on the religious and moral facets of US history.)

22) *World Magazine*; P.O. Box 420235, Palm Coast, FL 32142-0235 ; 386 447-6349; www.worldmag.com (The best source of alternative—non-liberal-biased—information I know of.)

23) And for those who want to hear from a 1960s radical who became a conservative: FrontPageMagazine.com (David Horowitz's web page.) Also: Center for the Study of Popular Culture, P.O. Box 130707, Houston, TX 77219-0707

Appendix 2

Young People's Guide to Success

The following list was submitted over the air waves by a caller to the Dr. Laura Schlessinger radio program.

1) Complete high school and any advanced education.
2) Live on your own for at least one year (college dorms do not count.)
3) Be at your career for at least two years.
4) Do all on this list and be at least 21 before you even consider getting married.
5) Pay off all debt before getting married (mortgages do not count, credit cards and loans do.)
6) Before becoming engaged, determine prospective spouse's religion; if it differs with yours, whose will you follow and under which will the children be raised?
7) Will the holidays be spent with both families, one or the other, neither or alternate?
8) Children: How many and what discipline will be used?

The woman who originally wrote these guidelines had several children. Those who followed them have had long, monogamous marriages. One daughter ignored them and her sister says she has lost track of how many marriages she has been through.

I highly recommend that any young person who gets this list keep it and review it once a month to stay on track. If you're really smart you'll memorize it and review it once a month.

(Memorization fades without the review for most of us.) Personally, I would add two numbers: (9) Abstain from sex before marriage; (10) If you are a Christian, do not marry outside the faith.

I confess, like so many coming of age in the 1960s, I did not follow these guidelines when I was young and it messed up a large part of my life until I was almost thirty and will have some residual negative consequences until the day I die. Don't make the same mistakes so many of us baby boomers made. This list, over a lifetime, may be one of the most important things you will ever need, but you must follow it for it to do any good.

SUPPLEMENTAL TIPS

In raising my own child, I would like to add one more resource: a battle plan. When you are a sophomore in high school, if you haven't already decided, choose what you want to be: a teacher, a lawyer, a doctor, a franchise owner, whatever. You might want to aim a little high; you can always lower your goals later. Keep in mind that it takes a lot of money to live nicely today. Then plan in detail how you will get there. Does it take a college education? You have to do well in high school to get to college. What skills will you need? How will you get them, where will you live, how will you get the money? Does the military offer such training and will they pay for your education after your service? Can your parents really afford to send you to college/trade school and support you while you get trained? Are you willing to get along with them so they will? If not, what is your alternative? It does not matter if a year or two down the road your goal changes. You can always review and change the battle plan and the goal, but to not plan is to plan for failure. "You can't steer a truck that isn't moving."

Keep in mind that the harder you work when you are young, on average, the better quality of life you will have when you are older. A teacher or a journeyman electrician can usually apply for higher paying jobs than a high school dropout.

Appendix 3

Political Contacts

1) The White House: telephone (202) 456-4114 FAX (202) 456-2461 e-mail president@whitehouse.gov

2) The Vice President's Office: telephone (202) 274-5000 FAX: (202) 456-2883 e-mail vice president@whitehouse.gov Vice President's Senate Office: telephone: (202) 224-2424

3) Congressmen and Senators: U.S. Capitol Switchboard: (202) 224-3121 e-mail for individual congressmen and senators can be found on the web at voter.com.

4) Write your congressmen/senators' contact information and write a list of local politicians and keep it where you can reach it and update it when necessary:

MEDIA WHO NEED TO HEAR FROM YOU:

1) ABC e-mail: http//abc.go.com/abc/help/contact.html

2) *Boston Globe* (617) 929-2000; editor (617) 929-3049

3) CBS (212) 975-4321

4) *Chicago Sun-Times*: (312) 321-3000

5) CNN (404) 827-1500

6) *Los Angeles Times*: (213) 237-7935 (opinion department) (213) 237-4511 and FAX (213) 237-7679 (letters to the editor); e-mail: www.latimes.com (follow prompts to e-mail windows)

7) NBC NBC-Nightly News: e-mail: Nightly@NBC.com

8) *New York Post*: (212) 930-8000

9) *New York Times*: 1-800-NYTimes; 500 7th Ave, 8th Floor, NY, NY 10018; www.newyorktimes.org

10) *USA Today*: (703) 276-3400; www.usatoday.com

Appendix 4

Free Speech at Risk

A Special Report from the Heritage Foundation:

Introduction: Talk radio, the Internet, Fox News, think tanks and grassroots organizations—can you imagine where conservatives would be today without these institutions? But these things did not always exist, and if many on the left have their way, conservatives will not have them available in the future.

For many years conservative ideas were shut out of the national political dialogue. The three television networks—CBS, NBC, and ABC—followed the liberal line on foreign policy, national defense, domestic policy, economics, and social issues. There were few conservative commentators or columnists. Talk radio was practically nonexistent. The major universities were increasingly left-wing.

Beginning with Barry Goldwater's defeat in the presidential election of 1964, conservatives began to think about how to reach the American people with conservative ideas. Slowly, over decades, conservatives built up alternative institutions to get around the blackout in the mainstream.

The Heritage Foundation and other think tanks were launched; they hired conservative experts who frequently could not get jobs in liberal-dominated universities, and began producing useful and principled policy ideas which have been adopted at a far higher rate than anything academia has produced.

Other conservatives learned how to use direct mail to reach conservatives with facts and ideas that the media shut out. Grass-roots conservatives were informed in this way about the handing over of the Panama Canal, the Equal Rights

Amendment, the abuses of the liberal Congress, and many more issues—and frequently changed the policy debates.

Conservative talk radio arose in the late 1980s, after the Reagan administration repealed the "Fairness Doctrine" that had discouraged broadcasters from putting controversial programming on the air. Cable television gave rise to Fox News, and with its success a demand for more conservative commentators on other television networks and cable channels.

Most recently, the Internet has given conservatives the ability to get out enormous amounts of information to the public, to hold the mainstream media to account, and to talk to each other. The 2004 presidential election might have turned out differently had it not been for the instant analysis of Dan Rather's fake memos that slammed President Bush right before the election, and the Internet-driven videos and ads that questioned Senator Kerry's war record.

Many of these avenues are now under attack. Unless conservatives recognize the threat to their ability to communicate with each other and with the rest of the American people, we could find the outlets we make best use of severely curtailed—while the Big Three networks, public broadcasting, the *New York Times*, the *Washington Post*, and other liberal media continue on their way unharmed. This report lays out some of the imminent threats to conservative speech and communications.

THE FAIRNESS DOCTRINE

The Fairness Doctrine was a government rule from 1949 to 1987 that had the opposite effect of what its name implies. It was supposed to create fair and balanced broadcasting by compelling radio and TV stations to air both sides of controversial issues. In practice, it led to most stations avoiding controversial content altogether. And some presidential administrations used the rule to harass conservative broadcasters and even force them off the air.

The FCC repealed the rule in 1987. And immediately conservative talk radio sprang up—with Rush Limbaugh leading the way, followed by G. Gordon Liddy, Michael Reagan, Sean Hannity, and hundreds of others nationally and locally.

The left was taken aback. Here for the first time was a media phenomenon they did not control. Their attempts at duplicating talk radio's success on the left have flopped again and again, even well-funded, highly publicized efforts.

Unable to compete, they complain that conservative dominance in talk radio isn't fair. So a number of leftists are waging a campaign to bring the government into the situation by reviving the Fairness Doctrine, which would enable them to force their way onto the airwaves.

The leftist media organization FAIR (Fairness and Accuracy in Reporting) has produced a position paper that complains of "the immense volume of unanswered conservative opinion heard on the airwaves." They quote with approval a complaint from a lawyer that "Political opinions expressed on talk radio are approaching the level of uniformity that would normally be achieved only in a totalitarian society."

A University of Michigan professor, Susan Douglas, has created a platform for "saving" America from conservatives. A key plank in her platform is recognizing "how important media reform is, particularly the reinstatement of the Fairness Doctrine...We see the results of too much Rush and O'Reilly without any balance: voters who don't have the facts."

This is far more than a campaign by left-wing cranks. Two FCC commissioners have recently called for some version of the Fairness Doctrine to be imposed. Members of Congress have introduced bills to bring back the rule. One measure almost made it through attached to another bill until some alert conservatives noticed the trickery and removed it. But the bill was reintroduced this year and is in Congress now.

Defeated presidential candidate John Kerry praised the Fairness Doctrine, saying: "You would have had a dramatic change in the discussion in this country had we still had a Fairness Doctrine in the course of the last campaign. But the absence of a Fairness Doctrine and the corporatization of the media has changed dramatically the ability of and the filter through which certain kinds of information get to the American people."

A consortium of liberal media groups is aggressively pushing an Internet-based petition drive to restore the Fairness Doctrine or its modern equivalent. The boards of advisors of these groups represent a virtual who's who of influential liberals. They are united in a well-funded drive to bring back the bad old days when Washington decided who could say what on America's public airwaves.

And this time there are many who want to extend the Fairness Doctrine's reach beyond the airwaves—to cable TV and satellite TV. Their main target is Fox News.

THE INTERNET

The Internet has significantly changed the way politics and policy-making are conducted in America. The mainstream media can no longer filter what citizens can learn, as a vast array of facts is at everyone's fingertips along with commentators from left to right who interpret the facts and give their opinions.

This free exchange of information is looked on with horror by some, especially those in the mainstream media who fear losing their monopoly. And those in Congress who have succeeded in shutting down much political speech and grassroots activity through the Campaign Finance Reform Act of 2002 do not want the Internet to escape their grasp.

The Campaign Finance Reform Act is difficult enough to apply to traditional political activities. It was intended to get big money out of politics—which it tried to accomplish by limiting everybody's political speech. But of course this is an impossible goal—there is too much at stake. In the 2004 elections big money was funneled to groups called 527s, such as the George Soros-funded groups America Coming Together (which spent $78 million) and the Media Fund ($54 million); and the conservative Swift Boats Veterans for Truth ($23 million). The Campaign Finance reform supporters consider these groups a loophole and are moving to ban them, thus further limiting political speech.

Similarly, these supporters moved quickly to make sure that the Internet wouldn't escape their control. The Federal Election

Commission (FEC) gave the Internet a pass during the 2004 elections. But the Campaign Finance reform supporters went to court, and in September a judge ruled the FEC had to issue regulations on Internet activities during election campaigns. There regulations will be in place for the 2006 election unless Congress makes it clear that is not its intention.

The Internet is still new and ever-changing. Regulations cannot cover everything that goes on. Besides being an unwarranted limitation of political speech, the regulations make it likely that many activities will be considered illegal and ordinary people will be put at risk of huge legal expenses, fines, and even prison.

Anything that helps a campaign can potentially be considered a contribution. Web sites link to campaign sites. Solitary individuals who publish blogs (web journals) praise candidates. College students, grandmothers, and schoolteachers forward emails to their friends that might have originated from a campaign. If these things are considered contributions, ordinary citizens will have to file the massive paperwork Campaign Finance Reform requires—an expensive proposition not in financial reach of the average person. If it is unclear whether these are contributions, citizens will be fearful to act. And if they are not contributions, the same players could very well go to court again to specify more actions as falling under the Campaign Finance Reform Act, and citizens could find themselves guilty retroactively.

CONGRESS'S ATTACKS ON NONPROFITS

The Heritage Foundation and other think tanks, grassroots foundations, legal defense groups, organizations that alert citizens to issues from education to immigration to tax policy, local and national charities, and all nonprofit associations are threatened by a move in Congress to vastly increase regulation of such groups.

It seems that some members of Congress believe that corruption is rampant among nonprofits, and increasing the paperwork will solve the problem. There is no evidence that either of these propositions is true. The Heritage Foundation, like all nonprofits, had to file extensive paperwork at our founding to earn our non-profit status; we produce reams of forms for the IRS every year. We, like other nonprofits, have had to undergo an IRS audit that was entirely unwarranted and cost us countless hours and hundreds of thousands of dollars, and went on for 5 years before it was settled.

Most nonprofits are small and could not afford this additional burden; they will simply go out of business and stop serving the local needs that so many of them take care of. Small grassroots conservative groups may likewise be driven out of existence, and others that are badly needed will never come into existence. The Heritage Foundation will have to take many dollars that should be used to further our mission of promoting free enterprise, limited government, individual freedom, traditional American values, and a strong national defense, and instead spend the money on lawyers and clerks to fill out piles of new IRS forms.

SOLUTIONS

Threats to our freedoms can be defeated when millions of Americans are alerted and speak out. This report can be copied and given out. It is available on the Internet at www.heritage.org/FreeSpeech, and can be printed out or e-mailed to friends, colleagues, talk shows, members of Congress, and anyone else. The report also provides links to other articles on the issues discussed here, if you want more detail.

You can also write letters based on the information in the report to members of Congress, newspapers, Internet forums, etc. If you have a Web site or a blog you can report on it and link to it.

Citizen action has stopped threats to our freedoms before—and it can again. It is up to you.

Appendix 5

The Bill of Rights

Amendment I.

Congress shall make no law respecting an establishment of religion, or prohibiting the free exercise thereof; or abridging the freedom of speech, or of the press, or the right of the people peaceably to assemble, and to petition the Government for a redress of grievances.

Amendment II.

A well regulated Militia, being necessary to the security of a free State, the right of the people to keep and bear Arms, shall not be infringed.

Amendment III.

No Soldier shall, in time of peace be quartered in any house, without the consent of the Owner, nor in time of war, but in a manner to be prescribed by law.

Amendment IV.

The right of the people to be secure in their persons, houses, papers, and effects, against unreasonable searches and seizures, shall not be violated, and no Warrants shall issue, but upon probable cause, supported by Oath or affirmation, and particularly describing the place to be searched, and the persons or things to be seized.

Amendment V.

No person shall be held to answer for a capital, or otherwise infamous crime, unless on a presentment or indictment of a Grand Jury, except in cases arising in the land or naval forces, or in the Militia, when in actual service in time of War or public danger; nor shall any person be subject for the same offence to be twice put in jeopardy of life or limb, nor shall be compelled in any criminal case to be a witness against himself, nor be deprived of life, liberty, or property, without due process of law; nor shall private property be taken for public use without just compensation.

Amendment VI.

In all criminal prosecutions, the accused shall enjoy the right to a speedy and public trial, by an impartial jury of the State and district wherein the crime shall have been committed; which district shall have been previously ascertained by law, and to be informed of the nature and cause of the accusation; to be confronted with the witnesses against him; to have compulsory process for obtaining witnesses in his favor, and to have the assistance of counsel for his defence.

Amendment VII.

In Suits at common law, where the value in controversy shall exceed twenty dollars, the right of trial by jury shall be preserved, and no fact tried by a jury shall be otherwise re-examined in any Court of the United States, than according to the rules of the common law.

Amendment VIII.

Excessive bail shall not be required, nor excessive fines imposed, nor cruel and unusual punishments inflicted.

Amendment IX.

The enumeration in the Constitution of certain rights shall not be construed to deny or disparage others retained by the people.

Amendment X.

The powers not delegated to the United States by the Constitution, nor prohibited by it to the States, are reserved to the States respectively, or to the people.

Are We Losing America?
Order Form

Postal orders: Smith
P.O. Box 8155
Scottsdale, AZ 85252-8155

Please send *Are We Losing America?* to:

Name: _____

Address: _____

City: _____   State: _____

Zip: _____   Telephone: (_____) _____

Book Price: $17.95

Shipping: $3.00 for the first book and $1.00 for each additional book to
cover shipping and handling within US, Canada, and Mexico.
International orders add $6.00 for the first book and $2.00 for
each additional book.

Or order from:
ACW Press
1200 HWY 231 South #273
Ozark, AL 36360

(800) 931-BOOK

or contact your local bookstore

Charge card orders: FaithWorks
(877) 323-4550